Motivated for the Cause

Books by the Same Author

Non-Fiction:

Virtuism: Philosophy and the Aesthetics of Virtue

The Experience of Hallucinations in Religious Practice

Exhausting the Interaction of Words: Computer-automated Brainstorming with the ParaMind Program

Hyperreligiosity: Identify and Overcoming Patterns of Religious Dysfunction

Grandiosity and the Empowerment of the Spiritual and Artistic

Fiction:

Motivated for the Cause

Cast the Jewels into the Sea of Your Soul
and Evoprayer

Computer-Generated Writing

Motivated for the Cause

R.S. Pearson

Telical Books
Seattle

Published by

Telical Books

P.O. Box 27401

Seattle, WA 98165-2401

U.S.A.

Library of Congress Cataloging-in-Publication Data

Pearson, Robert Scott.

Motivated for the Cause/ R.S. Pearson.

1st ed.

LC Control Number: 2007902633

Type of Material: Text (Book, Microform, Electronic, etc.)

ISBN: 978-0-9748139-3-6

First Edition

1 3 5 7 9 10 8 6 4 2

Preface

I hope to find a way through my writing to help make the true spirit of poetry more popular by what is called the antinovel. I didn't invent the term antinovel, but it is seldom heard. It basically means a literary form that has none of the conventions of the novel (a definition similar to the one from Websters). In a best-case scenario, excitement about the novelty of the "antinovel" concept would sell copies of poetic books, and thus give poetry more of a chance of becoming popular again. The antinovel can read like a novel, but it elicits a *ponderance* of statements that is usually only reserved for poetry. These books can be actually composed of poetry – poetry that has been taken out of verse form and put into paragraphs.

Fusing poetic language into prose gives us not just the benefit of both, but a synergy. This prose can even be rewritten as non-fiction essays in new vital directions. For those not aware of the extraordinary value of poetry, I suggest looking at the theory of the Romantics such as Novalis. Poetry used to have the value that disciplines like psychology have today, and it was often like a religion to the people. We face a time today when fewer and fewer people read poetry. Often the lyrics of the modern music people listen to have restricted subject matters. Some believe poetry is in a sad state, because of the lack of sales of books by serious poets. By hiding our poetry in the form of the novel, we may begin to rescue poetry, and in some way, rescue and enhance some of the best thoughts in society.

From age to age, the documents we pass on from generation to generation are very different in the literary forms they change into. Even poetry can be said to be many different literary forms within the one form known as "verse" or metrical poetry. The dialogs, such as those of Plato, are in a way a literary form unique for us, passed down twenty-five hundred years. The speeches of political leaders change in rhetoric and the formats they use over time. Who is to say because anti-novels seem so unusual today that they will not resemble a standard literary form in the future? This form seems to strip artifice away from the conventions of fiction and non-fiction alike. And there is always non-fiction in our fiction: all novelists are philosophers of life and this shows in their novels. In such a form as the antinovel, the novelist or poet as philosopher is given a free reign.

Perhaps by changing the form of literature, we will be able to introduce new content. To those exposed to the experimental in art and have a valuation of traditional spiritual values, there is no charm for ideas that seem to lead so many to an early death or their disempowerment. Many experimental artists are too late to be shocking, thinking that by exploring obscenity, blasphemy, misanthropy, or addiction they are making some kind of statement. Sadly, this artistic statement was made over 125 years ago and has been made far too often since then. We need a new art to free the spirit again, not paint portraits of the spirit in shackles.

-- 1 --

Is there no literature that will end the street riots of hate and street riots of power envy? Is there no literature that will produce the effect? If not, why do I want to write?

To attempt to produce an effect is the only honest answer.

It is said that some people are only nice to others so that they won't be hurt by them. Is this the effect I want to produce? Some might say that we write to justify the life we've been living, or to justify our intellect. What about wanting to write only for the sake of art? Is there a reason to write like others write, or is there only a reason to become a missionary and help the starving infected? Could I devote all my creative effort to writing about the reason behind virtue? Perhaps if I did I could help two people go out and help the starving infected.

Many are seen in condescended categories. Many are afraid of having any honest power. They would rather manipulate each other with calculated and polite scheming, pulling the wins out of each other's subliminal treasure chests. And this here, what I'm writing, is my scheming intending to be inciting.

I'm convinced that many are numbed to the call of virtue. If they were not, they could now just walk to nearby phones and volunteer their lives and resources to helping the starving and infected.

We have found our causes, we have found the cause of art. It is the disguise that a day at the beach or in the mountains could see through for weeks. What are our motivations? What is left for my pen to say? It must say much; it must fill this book!

I should introduce myself. The reasons for this become clear as I attempt to provoke you with my words. I am the one who was too young at the distribution of the great Western secular consciousness yet too old for the durations of the ball games. We can all be happy with such biological fulfillments but we rightly deserve our eternity (Did I just break rule number one?). This is one ground this work hopes to tread: after biology, what? Do we know what we think about that question?

As many say, we exchange words for life. What else is there to do? Biology? I could be the philosopher and say that the reason why no concrete answers about the noumenal are given is so that we can develop our reasoning power. That is being beyond biology. Perhaps, it is even a virtue. The world that has been laid down is beyond our reasoning power, because it is impossible to understand a thing that we can only see fractionally.

So, the forbidden question is: is this a good world or a bad world? Could we be so brave to be like a miserable, suffering soul, who when hearing that question could emphatically state, "It is a very good world." And they would not be saying it sarcastically.

What about the majority of humanity? How would the masses answer this question? I'd say that the majority of humanity is illiterate to the intricate problems of philosophy, but that's not to say I go around talking behind their backs, bad-mouthing the masses every chance I get. Are they qualified to answer the question or not? The most relativistic of all of us still has a concept of the virtuous. He, or she, judges their world by this concept. And the judgment they make, even "subconsciously", alters the world they judge, drastically.

We see so little of the noumenal. When we do look at philosophical material, skimming the surfaces of this or that, do we tend to just want to stop, eat, make a phone call, or whatever? 1'm sorry; I should not stereotype my reader. I'll try to be more careful.

If I am getting boring, fine, I won't always be here in this book in this explicit way. Regarding your assessment of this book and my talents as a writer, it is best to remember that all our present collection of literature, both ancient and modern, could be vanished and be replaced with totally different works -- just as good in every aspect. We have not reached any type of saturation point. The possibilities of the muses of literature are limitless. But then why is our literature so redundant?

I am not well-read enough to write a redundant book. With that statement in mind, will this be the book that gently documents the scream of the noumenal without conventional modernism? Let it be known that it is an attempt.

Our eyes now look down to the planet, and we choose to look in these four recognizable categories:

1. The literatures
2. The histories
3. The religions
4. The sciences

How are we to understand the world of these four? Where is our pen to begin anew?

With the literatures, that our young brave men and women, with brain-flowered pens exposed to our shores? Or the histories, that human nature revealed with its screams and its blood and its weak attempts at stifling? The religions, with the answers questions backwards in time until the fade melts? The sciences, with the obsession and the utilization of ultra-photography?

So, my dear models, where do I leave you with my pen -- with a nude dawn of a new emotion? What I do know is that the enrollment of yet another quarter in the schools will enclose our fresh young bloods to tell us of our lawns and cars and houses. The playground and swing sets of each hundred years document the history of our human natures. The church doors open to quiet lonely eyes from wandering; to ease our jaws from wracking our headframes. The sciences rip apart our vital areas to increase our potential for warmth.

I believe in the abstract. I trace the slight movements it makes. It makes these movements as a reaction to prayer, or when it is aware that I want to play a game with it. I fell in love with the abstract. It cared and cares for me still. It always hopes for the best. I know what the abstract is: it is the common Lord of mankind. It is the God of my childhood.

This God says "Call unto me and I will answer you, and show you great and mighty things that you have not known."

Our multiple-choice answer is:

A) Impossible. There is no God, there are no new colors to be shown to us.

B) Impossible. There is a God, yet I *have* seen all colors available.

C) Impossible. There is no God, but there are new colors, which I can find for myself

D) Possible. There is always a divine life. The concept of God is a little archaic in this age of Post-Freudian bliss, yet I have a healthy curiosity and I will call.

E) Possible. There is a God, but I am experienced. I will give God one-third and he will give me one-third in return. Otherwise, there is too much sacrifice for the viewing of the new colors.

Soon, I (or is it you), won't be here in this obvious way. I'll show up now and then; but, for the most part, you'll be on your own. But, for now, here I am and there you are. You might have real friends and you might not. You may live with your parents who you may or may not respect. You may be in your backyard garden or in a studio apartment. I doubt that you are helping the starving infected. I doubt this utterance disturbs you in any way. You'll be on the street rioting next Tuesday.

Strength, boundless virtue, creative youth; boundless love and passion for the air in their hair. Thoughtfulness, concern and compassion. Charity; boundless youthful ideals. Empty the mind, soak in the aesthetics of the outdoor environment.

Strength, boundless virtue. No cultural ties. Work good work. Die for one's God.

It's almost like I could say its O.K. to be the way we are, but I can't. We are neither the children we once were, nor are we the adults we had planned on being.

Pardon me, there I go stereotyping my reader.

Yes, I am not the child that I once was, nor am I the adult I planned on being. The reason for this has only to do with the law of niceness that I had originally set up and then gradually transgressed. Certain types of people in high places have often argued against this law, and their influence is felt in all of our lives. And by the way, I think there is a difference between being nice and being polite. I said nothing about being polite.

-- 2 --

The convenience stores, various shops, affordable modern paradise for the young consumer. All the strength returns upon knowing he can pay the price. Many months rent paid, food, sundries and clothing to last months also. And a car, gas and more money. But his loneliness doesn't end. The mood he would get was a heavy, gloomy feeling, like someone not quite relaxed, not quite at home. At times he didn't know if this was good or bad.

The cars go together with the jeans, faster than that, but not for the youth; the crust now lives. A society of personifications of television commercials lives close by. They have become the Animation of the Inanimates.

"Popular interest invested in our youth. Cultural virtues constantly leaving. In the trials of the future, will all faith run tired?"

Up before dawn, getting dressed, down the steps, on the public sidewalk I go. The town, in dark seems painted brown, I'm contained. Past an all night video game arcade . . . I could get a cup coffee there -- I've got the money now. I'm walking with ease -- what is there to see in a land with no memories? No dime store that I went to at age eight with what was once known as glee. The local, small shopping complex appeared to my mind before I understood capitalism. The stores were innocent and offering before me.

Memory lanes embroidered into the eternal. City parks and memories of people in the library fields. The days in a junior high. The kissing of a new season. The road runs long. The heart beats on.

(Etching in events. Cleansing regrets for new experience. Hopping aboard a decision's train. Opening up the door and walking outside).

Oh! The closeness of a childhood home! Where now? Are there any tricks that God can play on my present scenario, a wave of his mighty hand and I am a happy man? Instead, I imagine a thousand killing times:

"It's your fault human, it's all your fault. God can't help you. He won't care if you act like you do."

"But I can't help it, I really can't."

"I am a holy God. I will help you only if you don't resist the change."

"We have been working on it like this for years, there is such little progress."

"I think there has been much progress."

"But, there are lots of times I want to just die, if life on Earth will always be this boring. "

"That's right; you must die to yourself."

"I once loved this life. When I was a child, life was a joy. It seems that I was a different creature then, and the life was made of a different substance. There were acres of wilderness near my home and I had many close accessible friends. I've changed. I don't want to die, but I do want that which is dead in myself to live again."

"But, remember mystery, remember strength. These things don't have to be lost when you die to yourself."

I only want to choose the good, but...man, I get so tired. There are various factions thinking they must mold me for the better. The proposed, "God who is there" is doing all that He can. It is just that I am so ignorant. Most of the time, I feel He is working so slow, yet He expects me to be satisfied with what He is doing. I rarely am satisfied and then I feel I am walking after my own lusts -- that my soul's desires are held in ignorance of the True Life.

I've been walking for twenty minutes, and I could walk twenty minutes more and be at some docks. But, these docks are not like the docks at home. The town here has no class, yet is I who have developed complexes because of this lack. Could it be the change of the generations? Do I bring this spotlight with me?

What happened to my land! The terrain, the trees, groups of trees, grasses, bramble? Where is my field? Get me out of this urban mess! Where is the ground that brought forth the nourishment of my soul? Do I no longer deserve my landscape? Am I a new essence of human, lowered to a new classification: adult?

The fields of childhood -- further description would defile the intent. My way back to the past sometimes seems purely a financial question, yet this is only a symptom of the problem which I've acquired.

Poverty would not be so bad if you could travel around the world and sleep in communal housings and do an hour's labor everyday for cheap food. Idealism never stops. So be it; never stop. We need the practice. Freedom doesn't seem to be too good anymore -- if we are brought up in chains. Soon the prison really is in our hearts. Purity is the only way out. (Watch out for semantic prejudices). Holiness is for the gentle. Holiness is for the small.

This circus house of wanting, the swirls of oppressive function of human haste and hurl -- some flourish and are kept in waves of air surrounding, most are brisk and removed from their doubts. There is little real wisdom in store for those who see themselves as a carnival carnivore.

Places like this, they erode our facial structures which were genetically given. The members here, individual yet forming tissues of symbiotic structures of new tradition. There are earthly rounds, the eternal seasons, seasoning the manufactured world artfully. The dream of consumers just goes on and on. The fantasy of philosophers sings the same damning song. Enough for a chance for God? Will you now seek His rest, or continue in opinion of his supposed meaning? There is no reason for the saintly carnival to exist in our lives, yet I will continue to post up hand-bills for it all over my town and future towns.

Something is going on. The Earth is in a prefect state of balance, yet human life can be a mess with wars, car accidents, venereal disease and consciously malicious deeds. If the popular concept of God is true, then it is free will that has got us into all these problems. If the Hindu/Buddhist theory of reincarnation is true, then it is our pre-ordained Karma combined with free will.

Take one universe, one planet; existence: a light

that shines and gives light inside the eyes that see. The eyes that see are more than the burlap sacks of matter will ever be. Activate one trillion souls, over a period of hundreds of thousands of years of human growth. Allow the knowledge to be given, the judgment to reign high over all confusion centers: romance, money, sports, jobs. A home is a castle is a hide away for the tunnels of existence.

The end of this world comes in curious ways. As he finished urinating into the toilet he lifted his head and focused his eyes out the window. He noticed it was dark and lifted his hand to see it was only 4:45 PM on his watch.

"It's only 4:45 and its dark already? Seems like it's getting darker earlier every day. There are a lot of clouds, maybe that's why it's dark so early."

The next day, as he was walking home after playing baseball in the park, he noticed how dark it was.

"Four o'clock and it's almost pitch black. And there wasn't a cloud in the sky today."

That night he heard on the news that they were reporting the strange phenomenon. As the days passed by, it got darker and darker earlier and earlier until there was no more light at all.

Yes, here we are, now, back to each other's arms again. You softly say into my sweatered chest, "Espresso at the cafe at three?" No more to say to the unknown, no more to say to the patient winds of the Earth.

Come out with me like when we were fourteen, the rarest year of all human life. A gift, the gifted together we were censored outlaws, seasoned children together on the road and words, ideas, swirling around our red (mine) and blue (yours) jackets. Forgotten road with houses, lost in sequences of techno-progress -- it's still there where I remember it! I open the door to one of the houses and look into my early childhood.

A field of photographs, I seem to have stumbled upon. All deserve my time and attention. My time and attention desire them. But there's one there I sense, I've been eager to see it all my time. Forget common sense (that would be too good to true), the walls that ignorance erected has kept my life well away from you. (Though the prospect appears, in the name of abstinence, this revealing might not have been planned).

You come into the room, and the more rooms you enter in and sleep and stay and kiss and walk with me through the forest where we had stayed for days complete. The power of poem splashes around a mysterious word bath, while we adventure on the road with autumn air and temperature.

I saw a person with strangely beautiful facial features; a document from an unknown race. The skeletal, cartilage, and musculature structures of the face were exquisite, with the skin a tone of golden brown. Some faces are very rare, perhaps one in a thousand exhibit such an original appearance. They are not your common beauties, not glamorous, more like divine. These people's faces are the tools for expressing a wide range of emotions that may be lost to most of us. Perhaps some of these emotions are extremely rare, and require the proper facial musculature, for the facial expression that accompanies the emotion. I remember some odd emotions from childhood. My face has not since been exercised in such serenely alert positions.

Her: I save it for her. A million ocean dreams, a blue sun for filling out the dripping window rains. Lace, warmth, blanket scenes, a thousand memories with her in a land, an epoch during which we kiss the trees and climb. Nothing becomes of my memories of earth; they are undone.

Friends: running around games on the grass I play with them. For my life I would give; I would fight to the death for them, in a world where emotion means truth and actions are uneasily undone.

Myself: an eternity shopping for myself. Ceiling orange promenade, I go walking through bliss sustained, in memories of past compacted and fermented into finesse nostalgia. The proper aging of real time events.

Her, friends, and I. Grasses of blue, pink, and green grown in perfect rectangles on the ground, on the flat ground of a future front yard. I-Thou relationships through thirty million years of joy, pain, boredom, awe. So while you're here, mind, dance, sing, explore; become a historical personality. Don't fade in a minute and a half, squirt the paint out and move!

I knew my muse and she loved me more than any other. We were both artists in love with God and the universe of awe. How come we didn't grow up next to and with each other, my Little Lost Love? How many of you exist out there? Out there are forgotten Fridays (off for the weekend!). You never left me. I never insulted you. Perhaps, I'll go to a planet of you's when I die. Think of the days we could have spent together, so many days, so many weeks. You are not forgotten, although we have not yet met.

Days and nights out of the rain. Saturday spent in the clubhouse made of old woods that we found in the large fields near our houses. Poetry survives and opens virtuous eyes in us.

This love I'll never accomplish alone. I go up the front porch and ring the doorbell on an old friend's home. After dinner I go out again and play in the quiet suburban streets. I watch the cloudless sky's dusk. It is slightly blocked by telephone and electricity wires. The cooler air sets in. I wave goodbye to friends and go home...

"All aboard life game!" "Here!" We shout as it calls our names from the roster. God is good, oh, bound intellectuals, God protects like an older brother would. I know to you He seems too good to be true, but can't you believe all the testimonies that He is true?

Who wishes to be young right now? We can go back in time. "Verily," it is said, "Unless you enter heaven as a little child, you shall not enter in at all."

That is exactly what I've been waiting for. The Garden of Eden exists today at the supper table. The fruits of right and wrong are still upon the tree. Childhood naiveté blocks out all of what we know to be evil.

Struggling in error, walking and sleeping on empty pages, forgotten planet that holds mystery only for the eyes of the young. No one has been answered, no crowded street scenes of miracles, at least now. But, is Then factual data for the Present when it exists only in the Past? No guidebook written; we are devoid of an Earthly Owner's Manual. We are left naked behind priest's robes, professor's glasses, and bohemian regalia. No one knows but the mysterious occultists, who may reek of Satan, and who we dare not touch.

The bloated and weird, some say they feed the soil. Motivated for scum, for fleshly food, their dying bodies toil. The crusty heroes of earth, their demons remain loyal. For sex and tummies, their foot hits the shovel. For their lines and wrinkles, their foot hits the shovel. Their mysteries of mates and sports help feed the soil. They think it keeps some souls alive to continue to toil. A wondrous plan, the manic cycle sweeps away. The clock is ticking on and on; it's bright and spring and cheerful as we close our eyes.

Revolt! -- the prime of our reason, which now states the conclusion:

"Before the Bomb drops, I must say that the Earth was set up in such a way that no answers were given. Therefore, humanity's minds must not matter to whoever set up the Earth. It's like...how you would feel if you were not invited to your office Christmas party?"

"But we are here on Earth, already. We have plainly asked for truth. Besides, they went through all this time and money to set the earth up."

"But, did you ever figure that it was not set up for you?"

"For who, then? A snack-bar for microscopic animals, who feed on humanity, as we see it, in the form of diseases? For who, when we are perhaps playing the roles of cells, along with animals and plants in a large body similar to our own? For Who? Are we mere digestive organs, for the breakdown of the Earth's elements through ingestion, digestion, and excretion, for a reason far, far removed from us?"

-- 3 --

As children to the Father God is our purpose; to be cared for and to do wondrous deeds in seasons of increasing virtue, as we reflect, constantly cleansing the conscious mirror that is our soul. More and more I want reality to dawn on me, but there is a sunrise that I do not care to witness, a possible reality that I'm desperately hoping is not true.

To start with, you are a human whose heart of flesh will one day stop its incessant gifts of beating. With your death there is another death that will occur to the millions of creatures which compose yourself. You are a myriad of cells, in a vision of yourself in which they make, or help make, you one and alert.

The same patterning may go for a worldview that I think about every now and then. I would never think about it at all, but it seems it could be true! Now that science has proven the facts of microbiology, it seems that, one day, they find out that we are humancells in a large organism, with dogcells, birdcells, cowcells, treecells, and everything else alive compounded with a cell suffix. Respiratory, digestive, nervous, reproductive: all things we know about in biology has its parallels in this new science that I have called meta-biology: the study of planetary bodes as living creatures.

It seems that if all hope has no foundation, if we are merely mortals, if eternity is not the virtuous reason of creation, then to provide the function of a cell is the only reason we are here. As I say this, I am safe inside this huge creature, just like my brain cells are safe inside of me. This creature, as if you have not already guessed it, is our planet Earth.

In meta-biology, the planet is seen as evolving through the digestion of coarse matter into softer by the animal life living within it. This appears to us as solids moving into liquids then into gases. The sun is an example of a planet that has evolved. Planets might give birth to moons, such as could be seen in the case of Jupiter's red spot, which is three times the size of Earth at it's present gaseous state, has it's own center of gravity and is orbiting Jupiter. It is obvious that Jupiter and Saturn are similar to solar systems. The different life on Earth seems here to play a function. Part of our purpose may be to digest Earth's coarse elements into finer elements, but we also play role of the earth's brain cells. All the animals also play varying roles of brain cell function. All plants are digestive and respiratory organs.

Just as cells in our own bodies have individual lives, we are given individual lives inside (or on) the Earth, as long as we play our part. The brain of the Earth is thus able to roam around the Earth picking up different sensations and thoughts in different environments. Just as we store and think memories with our brain cells, it stores and thinks memories with us. This means that it has its own consciousness that is the totality of all our thought. This would not be allegorical. It would be capable of communication with others like it, both younger and older.

The human brain is so wonderful, we know so little about it. The brain cells see out the windows of the senses where the world shines through and an impression is stored. The brain cells may be looked at allegorically as micro-humans, but only where the cognitive life is concerned. These brain cells have lives of their own to live; their lives are singular or multiple impressions of our actual life.

Since each cell relies on a man for its function and consciousness, and each man relies on the earth in the same similar fashion, could the singular difference between the planets and the sun be that they are different species, or could it only be a matter of age? Do the cell types change drastically, possibly like the way dinosaurs may have changed into humans? If somehow ganglions of consciousness are connected together, galaxies would obviously be larger cells, capable of more intelligent life than a brain cell, man, or planet. As we are capable of being conscious of, or better, using all of our brain cells for certain functions, our earth is capable of using us for certain functions. Is a solar system, or even a galaxy, capable of being conscious with, or using for its functions, all of its solar systems, planets, planet's lifeforms, and so on?

Birds singing from tree to tree: I know you're cells. Cats upon the laps of humans: I know you're cells. Grasses and herbs in the ground, the dirt, the soft dirty hybrid dirt...the soil, carrying types of hormones of its being. Water: you are the plasma of the Earth. Stone: you are the bone of the Earth. Trees: you are the mighty lung-cells of the Earth. The sounds, the music, the literature, the paintings; the microscope particles of the non-allegorical beast.

The currents inside our Wall Street Journal, the pulse carrying its heart is all over its skin. (Actually, that's technically incorrect. The skin would actually be the ozone layers and orbital gravitational pull of the very outside of the planet). The empty space of the interstellar universe is filled with its speech and others'. The orbits of planets in a system are like ducks on a pond -- their outer rims are distant. The bodies in motion and activity, although to us they appear as still, or just going in circles. The games, learning, vacations -- of course, we can not know everything about it.

One big head floating out in space; one big chamber of imaginations. Pulses beating inside it at once; one single thought from it is the sum of all our thoughts from that moment. The logical progression of its idea may be our eternity and more.

People around you are like cells around cells in the animal or plant body. Are there other tissues we form? Cats, dogs and other large mammals, but especially domesticated cats and moreso dogs, have unusual effects upon the human. Observe a domesticated cat. If it is like most cats, it uses the human as a personal masseuse. Those who don't like cats might say it exploits the human to pet and feed it.

Meta-biology can easily fill the gap of the enigmatic meta-pattern. The meta-pattern is the unifying pattern that ties in humanity with the Earth, the Earth with the solar system, the solar system with the galaxy, and the galaxy with the universe. What I am here proposing I do not know to be true, but as far as I can see, it is feasible. The consciousness of the human brain may be the product of the consciousness of billions of cells. The consciousness of the earth may be the sum of billions of humans and animals. Somehow, the ganglions can be connected: the pattern is in the airwaves.

Well, if all Earthly ganglia are connected in some strange way, then there is a larger world going on, around and outside, than you could ever imagine!

Our body's cells have less will and vision than us. Even we have limited will and vision. Could we truly be resources for a world we do not see?

If I could be near it in a mental way, I'd want to know some things. Just as we were once not aware of our cells inside of us, it may not be aware of us inside of it. Even if it was aware of me, how could I ever talk to it? It would be like one single stream of electrical charge in relation to the connected printed circuits of continents of super-computers. But, as we compose part of it, and our world is inside of it, our world is it. All of what we will ever feel or do or try may be needed to provide the maintenance of its life; the very structure of being for it.

Isn't it weird to carry your baggage -- your brains, your intestines, lungs, veins and so on around?

"I'm just carrying it around."

Use it!

How could we not use it?

Humans come and go, compromising unlovingly the singular truth of their existence. This soul writing this is still lovingly looking for one of the technician's manuals to the universe, and this pessimistic world view is a very likely possibility for the reason for human, animal, and plant life. The words of God that actually did save my soul still says, "Lean not on your own understanding."

Must I not "lean" on my own understanding when so many other humans are leaning on theirs? In deciphering this strange possibility, I have outshined the most reductive and formalized of intellects, the most brazen and smugly abrasive modern artist!

Why did I say this worldview is pessimistic? Well, I guess because it's so flesh oriented and not very spirit oriented. Everyone knows how mortal and corruptible flesh is. Maybe the lokas of the Hindu system are organisms too. Maybe the worlds have a cell exchange program. I doubt our own body's cells are somehow immortal, does our planet doubt that we are immortal? After what we've done to it, it...

A new type of metaphysics would be born if we saw the Earth as an organism, and us as cells within it, and the evil as the ones who try to keep us as complacent cells in this being, and God and Jesus as the ones who try to remove us out of it by our acts of virtue in attitude and deed. By our not playing a mechanical function, that is by our not being constantly self centered, not taking the marks of our own beast, but by being God-centered, and other-centered, we could arise out of the patterning that hinders us tremendously.

Perhaps the common ascetics were right when

they made their sacrifices. They may, or may not, have freed themselves from being a human-cell in this organism. A pessimistic view would think that perhaps the planet views these cells as being a type of abnormal cell, and that is why we're hindered when it comes to spiritual growth: too many free ascetics could be dangerous to the planet, there could be no more proper functioning. A spiritual view, and which seems obviously more correct, would see the freed people as more beneficial to the planet as a whole, and a lack of those types, that free quality in a large percentage of humanity, would be harmful to the planet.

If all this is not factual, one lesson may be learned from it: the only way to prove the existence of life on other planets, without actually seeing it, is to prove the necessity for it scientifically.

The Harvest of Souls, the Food Chain Myth unfolds. Just why are we here? Wheat from the chaff? All has been sowed. I'm turning into gold.

-- 4 --

Slowly in pieces. One by day by day by day by one day of singular achievement. There are days of similar slothfulness. The way that you've got to look at it is that there will be millions of inventions after you're dead. You don't want to miss out. So the more you invent, the less you'll miss.

A dictionary's keyboard tapped into our melancholy emits nine-hundred new words which are transformed into chromosomes which effortlessly, fully, perfunctorily, fill out the organism which the genes predict. The organisms are obviously poems, short stories, novels, manuals and other types of books. But is that all they are? Surely, we can see our own replete plates on the dinner table in front of us! I will elaborate further on this.

Imagine a fish tank with tropical fish and pure water. Then imagine pouring in a small bit of pink dye into the water ever day for two months. This pigment would be of a type such that the fish would not be hurt and also be saturated with the pigment.

Second, imagine every particle of matter is actually a type of vibration and it began to become vibrated at one-and-one-tenth times its current "pitch." Everything would be in the same relationship as it was previously but if one creature was taken out before the rise in pitch occurred, and was placed back in the landscape after the change occurred -- it would notice a difference.

Now connect these two examples with their preceding paragraph. After this settles, connect the new combination with the words pragmatism, virtue, orthodoxy, and truth. You have just seen something very rare upon the Earth.

Poets! Do the world a big favor: start writing textbooks, instruction manuals, and encyclopedias on the nature of the other half. Examine it like a textbook. Can you be so large? Science has too long held the monopoly of luscious organization. A Table of Contents outlines more than we could ever produce, but which we will produce in spite of what praised pessimistic intellects who have digested themselves attempt to infringe on our neo-intelligensic playgrounds.

Inside the dumb chamber of utopianistic art, home maintenance, extensive vegetation. Extend the vegetation: grow it all over the house and yard. Freak out the neighbors, create a reputation. Grow it in convenient spaces. Extend vegetation constantly to keep the world's oxygen at a higher level.

"Occasionally, not very often, you'll hear some artist or poet talk about an unearthly fruit, like a cross between a strawberry and a watermelon, or a cross between a papaya and grape. Well, somehow I got hold of some unearthly fruit; I got enough to last me months. I really thought they were great for the first few days, but, you know, eventually I'd leave some half uneaten in the refrigerator, and some of them ended up to ripe too eat after the first month. I guess it's like anything else, the magic can wear off."

"Millions of tinted notes of smell sweetened my

bedroom upon awakening, one morning. A heavenly device, it reminded me of the flower petal rains that surprised us all one morning. The scents in general reminded us of the synthetic candies that we used to eat on the Earth as children; it refreshed me of our small purchases and sensuous savoring. The showers of smells were so bright, meticulous and moist, my nose was breathing so slow and softly. I never woke up in quite this way before, yet the mornings never were the average part of the day. One morning the sun was seen through the ceiling of my room, on the first floor of a ten-story building! Some mornings, granted, are much less interesting, such as the minor things as finding breakfast on the nightstand by one's bed."

Walnut and silver are the thought contents around your castle in blue skies. Conveyer belt to the turning point. Continual blastings of beautied open. In hazy heat, oak grove trees spreading in orange refreshments and orange globular architecture is meshed in between the trees for maximum oxygen efficiency. Furlongs ahead of the eternal next month away from death's progress, hounds crypt Neptune and its magma of blues. Turquoise -- other planets as organisms. Realities that are none of my business.

Orange globular architecture, again all against the blue sky. Standing on blackish purple ground, with peach and lavender pebbles, I am breathing this in heaven after being here a mere eternity.

Robotic groundwork maze, purposeful efficient fun, works quicker than that, apogee form of run! Puddles and gravel and a little boy sitting nearby with a rubber space monster doll.

The openness of heaven, yet contains all the "elite's" souls; perhaps we will have planets where twenty of us might stay. The infiniteness of creation is our eternal inheritance. The pondering of glory brings assimilation of it into our being. After God paid the price we gained permission. We were agreeably hid and disregarded under God's glory.

Pondering heaven, what can we not do there? Beyond what we can imagine as technology, the architects of a galaxy, they could be we one day. With flavors and textures and color, scent and sound, and five or six others, imaginations burst unwound. I hope for the eternal present to elapse softly, or cascadingly, in a river current, or aloft in gentle air breezes.

Now we are all here, and then we are all dead. We hope in You, oh Lord!

--5--

A thousand parches of summer, pebbles and sand on street sides, a rocky tan soft-hard soil crumbles under pressure from hands and feet. We unite the street stories, houses surround our streets.

Play out in the streets, be not afraid, cultured adults! Mystical sequencer, open the doors and quench our various thirsts.

I may again live as well as the memories indicate. I just remembered: the heart beats on; the road runs long.

Privacy on a flat land. Should it mean that much? Than, than, than. Comparisons always forget to lift that clutch.

The journey is like eating delicious foods. Reflect on current love all around. Are you safe now? Just for this moment? Reflect upon current love all around.

Some of their lives must be such a bore, already processed and packaged, routined and telecasted; selected activities for the young married couple. Should we hope they find satisfaction with a life that they presume they already know everything about, forty years before it ends? Will they have painful despair, should we hope they do?

They are busy fulfilling biology. They succumb constantly to the biological impulse and the behavioralistic impulse. However, this might not be all that bad; I believe in preference. If someone enjoys being average, is that a bad thing? Do the majority state that they are average? The average may enjoy themselves more than the artist. What type of qualitative comparison am I making?

Owned by us were I and you. We never wanted the future to play its game of chance to threaten the present. A rare season for mortals, a common memory for them. Economy ruins our horizons, another day of coming dusk. But, the winds' dusk are a beautiful sight-taste-touch-smell-sound. All five senses blend me at once. Sense perceptions I'm looking forward to in heaven.

Heaven is a thousand desires happening everyday, that before, and till the moment they reoccur, were lost.

It's not unusual to want to go out at any time, to live any place. But must we scrounge to feed our roots?

Sweetness decline, a modern supper at home; no air-raids, letting memories die...that I've outgrown? No fun on bicycles. I've moved to a new hometown. Too many hills. Seeking that plateau of my native land, doesn't my patron know what he is doing?

We indissoluble, no reliance on a chance for not. Unable, no lie, some work harder and are blessed with a curiosity not cursed with a ______.

Zero home paste, canvas forgotten. Hopeful but depressed -- the paradox. Actually, I don't get depressed anymore; I just get angry. I don't know if this is better or worse. After this, I'll probably learn patience.

Several parallel universes, there are thousands of ones with musical feelings. There are hundreds of variations of mellowness, of indignation, of exuberance. Aspects of the sustain, shift our transitions into countries: I am washed.

Listening to a documentation of Certain Chord Progressions, I imagine that all over the world, all over the time, there are a few who saw the loveliest chord progressions, and therefore have the inalienable right to write a book. Singing lovely songs against backdrops. Melodic structures of effortless recharge.

You see, we missed entirely. We started off talking about virtue and then digressed to art and then digressing further until the bottom line was ego. It wasn't even that sequential. Let's avoid doing it constantly. Let's attempt to regain interest in the virtuous -- it was our original pursuit. So, I must catch myself before the acts are created, to shout out about things that are wrong.

Why do you stand so far away, you can't see what's going on over here -- come closer.

Is there really anything called Help? Is there anything we can do to help anyone, or do we all die a mortal's death? Some people don't see that as the bottom line, but I do. Shall we help the immortal human or not? Another way of peering at life and hope.

There was a young man who thought he could help calm the belligerent nature of some people by this song he wrote. He worked hard on the arrangement and chose his words and their intonation with extreme care. He was doing something specific to help people. How simple! The specific people were affected for the better.

Another went through many pains her whole life. By types of effortless introspections, she was eventfully able to be bold, bold enough to go downtown and educate the alcoholics on the street. She was greater in courage than any other I have seen.

Proclaim in front of the most potent Van der Graaf generators the immortal doctrine of embarrassment; make it known. You won't be affected at all, they will think that you cringe inside as they would if in such an embarrassing situation. Their excessive tendency towards, and great fear of embarrassment, is only due to their insidiously misplaced egotism. But still, we are motivated for the cause of virtue. Change lives by embarrassing yourself in front of them. Heal the sick, encourage the feeble, feed the hungry, by accumulating these strange mental energies from others.

One is only embarrassed if one embarrasses oneself; shaming comes from inside. Few realize this pragmatically. When you are no longer easily embarrassed, you will have gained new power. The psychotic frame of reference may enter in; caution is advised.

Perhaps the revelation of this is too sacred, too potent -- only revealed under confined initiation.

We can all do things in the future if we pay the price, time and patience, in every aspect of our lives. Salvation; saving.

-- 6 --

The idea of his faith not being true opens wider the floodgate of secular beauties. The streams gush in. A Halloween at home and housewife: mystical, ethical, sexual. Bloated millions may not be mine. Should I believe in the skeletal future: our skeletal future?

The faithful stand firm in trial, and though I have not yet denial, how many desires of my heart are coming though? Although through poetic license, and genetically-encoded good intention, the remaining suspicions are few.

I start out strong (asceticism or grace?) to look with objectivity (optimism or pessimism?) on the seas of proposed wisdom (reincarnation or hell?). There are harbors of contradiction (poor or rich?), and sometimes they don't even agree with themselves (friend or foe?).

And so much good Christ did for me today, yet now again I feel empty. Does Christ live here in Braintown? And the Alchemy of Soul can be another hole, empty and alone is that truth.

A friendly girl crossed my midst. I refused her company. A prescribed muse is too jealous. Existence, you've won, you're winning.

There never was a game. Existence, you're winning.

Hey, damn it, why is reality like "this"? It is not our fault. If every human on Earth got down on his hands and knees, and prayed to God, would He end the charade? Could He open up the shop for good -- for at least five minutes while I get a pack of batteries? If every human on Earth prayed to God at the same time, would God then pull up the curtain and start the show?

And the TV and radio news proclaimed, "the rapist was set free on bail reduced to ten thousand dollars." God will set straight. If God doesn't set straight, then this reality exists, unchanged as we now see it. If God does set things straight, then this reality is not as we now see it.

Nutrition is secondary. Hairstyle is secondary. Teeth are secondary. A spouse is secondary. A home is secondary. Self-esteem is secondary... if the promises of the ways of God are what they say they are.

I traveled to glorify myself by creating my own immortality. I seemed to curse others who cared for me the most. I saw those as ignorant who were on the finest path. I was misled. I misled myself as much as others. The first thing You did was to accept me. The second thing You did was to lead me out of the religions of insanity. The third thing You did was to tell me the truth. The fourth thing You did was life itself.

Addictions of lust lasting forever? Even though the change came into life and heart? I continue in my iniquity and claim to know God. I'm pretty sure God is carrying me through. You say we can't know God and continue in sin. You think you've shed your skin of sin?

Believe not the damned; it's never been a good idea. Their plagues shall not be upon you, if you can care about your end. He that gathers in summer is wise. Turn not your ear from another human's cries. Bring them into house appointed for all the living. The light no man can approach, yet it approves of all things excellent: it is a gift. How could we pay for it? What would we use for currency?

A friend closer than a brother. None on earth we desire besides You. To this end, we were born. Save us from the chaff, the lies, the scorn. Save us from the chaff, the lies, the scorn.

What is there to be experienced in opening the door; I'm opening the door. Waiting on You in more ways than one. Impatient and bored. A sudden exposure might crisp my cells, my eyes are too wet. Someone with too much hairspray got to the blessings first; some miracle-selling millionaire is poor in spirit.

Art is outlawed in your town. Fresh cooked chicken receives my frown, in a Southern kitchen, in a Southern town.

TV evangelist bless my bowl, empty me of my filthy lucre; urine test of my soul, open my allowance. Atheistic humanism seminar, I see my mother there, I see her in her secret car. The modern school steals her heart, and gives her new recipes. The signs of the times are standing still within viewing range.

Through an entire Earth's existence resisting temptation common, Christ fell not once in view of the final production of souls for eternal redemption, by the contamination of God for us. While a certain group of Christ's followers say they can be sinless because now they know not to sin, so they don't do it anymore, making God's work seem like just a good upbringing. The transfusion of Christ's blood to ours – God's saved us by taking in the bad, and giving out the good. We can live with God's blood in our veins. We circulate God's blood in my veins. We are washed.

Flowers blossom and then fade away. Branches fall off trees in the storm. The learning of man gets outdated. But my love will never corpse. There are more of us that don't know You than the ones of us that do. It seems impossible for them to change. The lies that carry them are soon through.

Habit is gluttonously blocking out that which seeks to be preferred. The world around me wants to create me more than I will have created it. God opens his arms to me, but I sometimes know of no welcome since I hold up cardboard images of "Him" in front of God. These cardboard images are given to me by arbitrary and crass ideas. The dream is to be at peace. The dream is to be restful sheep? Like a sixteen-year old cat at serene rest on its owner's lap, we are told to cast all our cares upon God and He will care for them.

Recalling the pastimes we used to do. There is no substance to them now. Understanding the waste of time; we just live now like all the rest. Mutually submissive, I guess that sums it up. Weaken our wills and open us up anew. The war never ends and true peace never begins. But I'm beginning to learn how to wait for You.

When sunken into darkness, there is something inside me that is the proof of the change. The ugly realities can't affect it, but they can sometimes affect me. We all know about opening the door and the supper, perfect nondescript metaphor. Why do people also imply things more clearly, like "turn or burn?"

Blue promises never seconds away -- always later. Days turn into years into heaven's promises for the faithful. My mind is alive; my heart seems half-dead. I am forever in the test tube until death, in the puzzle that will not be solved until the death of the individual pieces.

We get rewards when we are acting the part. We find results when we shape to the mold. I've got very little to emphasize except life can be a waste of time, because if Heaven is so much better, and I know I believe the right stuff . . . this party boat is anchored.

The truth helps and the truth hurts; the rain cools and the rain whelps. You can't buy God's love with money, but there are some things that it does cost. It requires patience, and a meticulous reflection on how great life in God is.

Now, if we had the keys to the universe, we'd make it a sunny breezy day in autumn or spring. We'd connect each man with each woman, and make energetic toys for the puppies.

What we wish for from philosophy is not to study man's wisdom, but the revealed wisdom from the source of all wisdom. Whatever this source may be, one thing is for certain: it's probably not man! Man gets his own wisdom from the level of his intellect's capacity, or better yet, perhaps if these semantics are friendlier, his own soul's understanding. It seems clear from history that beyond a certain point, logic stops and one's own preference begins.

So with all seriousness imaginable, we must ask ourselves: is it true that truth can only be found by intellectual discovery, a progression in the realm of human idea, or is there something on earth in which the source of wisdom has revealed itself clearly?

I expect You to fulfill every selfish whim that comes my way and of course You don't. This makes me get angry at You (thank You for not getting angry at me!) I thought that You keep me poor, but yet You help fulfill all my needs -- more than the starving and the cold. Make me content, keep me in patience, so then my mouth won't lie and I will see life's glory.

--7--

All over the different galaxies, we are created in the image of God. We exist in a type of qualitative aspect of this image. This is not a physical image. And, the strangers, like on earth, but except in a different galaxy (even the closest far enough for me), the strangers are no different from you or me, because an eye is an eye; a soul is a soul.

We took the child with the Cri du Chat syndrome upon a stand, and asked him, tried to understand all that we could gather from inside us, about him. Such a rare child, in first twenty years this syndrome had been isolated, only nine cases had been observed. And here we have one to be kind to. The syndrome produces humans with a round, moonlike face, physical and mental retardation, and a weak plaintive cry, hence the name Cri du Chat, "Cry of a Cat."

Oh, Cri du Chat child, from where do you come? Do you come from the same factory that produced the rest of us? Do you somehow deserve your odd appearance and manner? All the mysteries of life are imprisoned in you.

The biological accident has made an unalterable impression on your soul. For some the impression is too bright, and to think the evil would destroy you like a twenty-year old cancerous dog. All in the name of their twisted idea of goodness, no less!

You are beyond the animals in every respect. To say human life is not beyond the value of animal life would cause too much weight to come crashing down upon the spine of my conscience. None of you have been given the chance to mature by one who understands you. I would not treat you like they have treated you -- even though some may have had good intentions.

I expire my muscle's obligatory responses when I hear the way the strong treat the weak.

I arise in my indignation only to smile at the back of God who is approaching the scenes, already having the retribution meticulously allotted.

The concept of humans born with different bodies on this sun baked shore, the vastly different, many humans of yore. The vastly different, we keep them hidden. God in His mercy has given us the vastly different to confuse the matters more, to build higher our minds and hearts.

When we see humanity meaning more than idea, the obvious virtues shine through. When we destroy all expectations of sociological organization and just learn to care for the needs of our moments and the planet's and its seasonal regeneration.

When all humans who desire it find a loving spouse. When all humans keep the doors of what we now call youth open. When the scientists reconsider much of the work they are doing and do an about-face to save the planet. When a concentrated effort has been made to fix what is broken.

When we can actually begin to ascend the pyramids and inverted pyramids of imagination. When our imaginations are heart-trained in the sciences, ethics, and aesthetics. When we have begun to take seriously the idea of documentation and supporting originality in the information of the imagination. When our hope is used to keep the doors of imagination open.

When all these things happen, we will be on a different planet.

Down here, the huddling pool, names of some of our most sacred characters. Down, down, the huddling pool, the more the planets, the millions of more existences, the ways of patchwork communications mutating our lives for the better. The more of the planets, the millions more of the planets: keep quiet! The earth, the inner layer; here we are. Within the billions of existences also exist millions; the cell theory -- cell liberation.

It starts out this way. Along the days in a course I was on, I made mistakes. I didn't confess the tangents, and excuses were made. I left the faith and sought out the myriad of systems utilizing the joyous methods of philosophical improvisation.

But today my thoughts are different. I see the truth as something that can't be just improvised. The truth exists regardless of any type of relationship we have pretensions of having with it.

Here are some of my possible conclusions:

(A) This is a school, and we must survive the theological confusion of this stage of existence. The earth's lack of absolute data concerning philosophical questions is ordained for a reason. The reason being that we must go through stages of personal reasoning and the search is the important process.

(B) The Christian idea of the wheat and the chaff is true. There is a monotheistic force that created our lives at least for His and our pleasure, but to enable our souls to be complete, He gave us free will thus enabling Him to have the companionship and interest of a free creature.

(C) All life is both supporting a larger life and also enjoying its own smaller existence. The cells of our body enjoy acting out the programming that they possess -- perhaps as much as we can enjoy the programming that we possess.

Which is true? Can only one be true? Which one? Does it matter? It is reality that is going on. Does it matter if I know which of my versions of the-reality-that-is-going-on is more correct? Will reality affect us all in the same way, and will it really matter?

One thing is certain: that the fulfillment of pleasure is a major factor in the meaning of life -- do the lessons we learn come as a by-product?

We seem to forget though that we have knowledge and even seem to have understanding. We are not wise beings though, and to top this off, it seems the dummies are in charge of the Earth. Why are the dummies in charge of Earth? Is that something the Earth does to whoever happens to be in power at the time? Does the Earth metamorphose all nations' leaders into the selfish and numb with no appreciation of the aesthetics of virtue? It seems the history of our world is a shining example of the world's power given to the wrong people.

Is the only way to look at this problem only in human psychology? Is that which makes a person want to be a powerful politician the agent that will intrinsically make them a bad force in world? It is said that the types of people who seek power most make the worst leaders. To give anyone this power of politics seems dangerous, albeit needful, in the first place.

We are in need of stupendous revelations in common sense.

Anyway, to be happy is so important, yet to screw up your lifetime by not giving religion and philosophy an important place is very bad. Many people that thought religion and philosophy are only contrived for selfish purposes -- to make one feel better -- have found out that half of the time they do the opposite. Moment by moment, we must seek the truth, and realize human psychology. We put some emphases on our own psychology so it does not cloud the glory of whatever is the noumenal.

The danger of being alive is the danger of being accountable to a righteous judgment. As one philosophical school attempts to prove its predecessors incorrect and each new school stands on this ground -- that it is right and others are wrong -- we can now detect that the doctrines that are "culturally" called false are not necessarily false. They are being pushed aside by a mechanism that doesn't give them a chance in the first place. Some things obviously do progress.

I have learned it was silly not to think that there was One hearing my prayers. I have learned that it was silly for not believing in a God. Why? Because it is such a major either/or type of decision in all of our lives and a simple vote for atheism is senseless compared to the possibilities of getting an answer from this God.

Did I get an answer from this God?

I believe I did.

--8--

The only thing that will hold us back from enjoying a beautiful, technological and environmental future is that humanity will not be virtuous. Space flight is possible in its fullest extreme if virtue is humanity's guiding light. To build spacecraft capable of supporting a thousand humans is already within humanity's reach, but instead humans are preoccupied with destruction and mediocrity. Mediocrity is what must be destroyed -- everything in moderation -- but what that everything currently is must be expanded.

I don't want to waste my efforts in repeating the mundane. When the vision dies, the people perish by the mechanism of paranoid mediocrity.

If you have that love in your life and you know what friends are for, come over here and we'll play all right. We'll diminish and we won't keep score. Seasons like this we've had in the past, and seasons like this, you know, they may not last.

Realize this and they'll come back some more.

There might be a new science that could better describe the successful among us who retain certain aspects of childhood and who do not indoctrinate themselves into every aspect of the status-quo adulthood. Perhaps, people could devise a new term for individuals who rejected many aspects of the adult mentality in both rebellion and conformity, while retaining their sanity and social interface-ability. The term "eccentric" or "genius" just won't do.

Three generations from now, the people for whom I raise my brow. Away, away, oh current day, I spoke again my seeming hay. I ask of you, do I beg of you, oh future humans: speak to me, too.

If this life is a breeding ground for souls, then examine the polemic against experimentation for its own sake, and the pluses of virtue.

Can there be non-violent explosions on page? If there are any, I hope some will leak out into my life.

Crank call, ring and run. Money rains from a friendlier sky. The discipline of the Spirit is to make me better. Oh, how I shall be that day!

"Yes, most people really don't understand. There is some natural law that works in the realm of self-image and being at peace. Most people don't understand that you've got to love being a wimp to always be at peace with yourself. Some coat their relationships with a power that is false to each other. People that are truly free of the worst in life may be enslaved to a self-confidence problem; they accept the truths that humility brings."

They had mapped out the brain and the cells that did what, they had spoken a science, wishing a pleasure -- the technique of dream planning was not in its infancy. By certain chemical compounds, and certain electrical messages, they revived some vivid childhood, adolescent, and young adult memories, in slightly forgetful two-hundred-some-odd-year old man.

One day they will have a phone, that is, they (who are they?) will have a communication device that can transfer sight, sound, taste, smell, and touch. I was thinking of putting flower petals of various kinds that I find in my yard and in the woods in a jar before they evaporated away. I thought: how could I communicate to someone how beautiful this was? My mind was altered into a beautiful smelling future.

Magnificent airplane of the Forty-Second century -- the future will always exist. Expand wing. You are always the same, now be glad. Optimum loved one: reality is always vigorous. Illusion is fragile. Journey into your colored future. Journey into your colored past. Stupendous building of the Thirty-First century -- virtue also exists in the past. Don't be deceived, you saw five years ago like you saw now. You are always the same. Now be glad. Horrible war of the Twenty-Seventh century -- another tale of science fiction? Is any more than this real to us?

If this future does exist, what a load of information mankind will have stored. Intricate indexes of discs, of cartoons, news programs, situation comedies, and a multitude of documentaries. Five hundred years from now, if the masses don't try to be one individual, putting all their eggs in one basket, there will be much information.

And what will you do, oh, pop theologian, when the flowers' eyes find your Armageddon lies out? When the future stumbles onto the barber's chair and gets cropped in the latest hairdo, what shall you then do? Three hundred years will elapse like the three hundred that just have, and mankind still alive in the course of the merciful justice.

--9--

Too many head-trips going on? Thinking about qualities that don't exist? About vacant situations, or empty encounters? None of that overpowers me, although I went through seasons when it did.

Yesterdays and the days before were summer dreams in love united, with crisp cool iceberg lettuce winter days that we were younger in. Times like this is when the poetry flows. I understand my salvation and I understand my cardinal sin: the sin of hypocrisy. The poetry flows because I am created in the image of God by the act of the Spirit, breaking the chains of sin, death, and hell. I confess past imperfections -- but all of me is of the Spirit right now, and sin consciousness, the pondering of sins, will ruin all that I have gained by having the Spirit living within.

In my path to God, I have found that I am not to exalt myself above other men to Godhead, but to understand that God loves me and cares for my soul even more than I ever can.

Outside human philosophy conclusions, to see all things outside of our human categories. Man, the subordinate of depth, despair and hairstyles. Planet Earth, planet Earth, planet Earth -- won't anyone speak to planet Earth?

"But God did, young son."

We are on a train that requires tickets all along the way down the track, not just at the beginning.

It almost happened: despair. Something I did, I

thought was a failure. Yet, I caught it, and examined the situation, and saw I could fight it.

There is time amongst me and a place where there is no poetry nor music, no philosophy nor art. This is a season caused by a Stuffed Belly. There is a season of strength, caused by documented fantasy, strenuous sobriety. This breaks through the numbness, drenching it for days. Hope is in these periods, and hope is always to be found.

We should have mercy on those who give us mean looks. We should not go after those who want us to know that they look down on us. They fuel up on every slander, considering maliciousness deliciousness. We should not cast our pearls before swine, to receive an opinion of our pearls that leaves a harmful memory.

Attitudes of dissatisfaction, the attitudes are a season. Opposite in their lives rarely, the season of acceptance. Acceptance brings pleasure, even if reality is not perfect. Although accepting imperfection in some areas is not what the wise care to do.

Trapped in the Self-Help Destruction Chamber, I've feasted on areas of my deadness. Sturdy areas of past enlightenment (if seen in a good light), are eaten by the promise of a fresh start.

"Have you heard about smile therapy? Up they go, sagging muscles need a lift. Let's face it, life's constants aren't always worthy of the pleasure which brings its crown, a smile. And the kinesiologists say, "It's good for you." Holding up a smile for five to ten minutes is like depositing money in the bank.

"Common experience in smile therapy is to get a burst of smile depthening charges. Similar to the laugh, but not laughter. Common experience in smile therapy is to gain clarity of vision, and a pleasant feeling of light. Shivering sensations are common to humans who practice smile therapy for more than five minutes a day. Partial reconstruction of youthful facial features is possible by the strengthening of the facial musculature."

Adept at rerouting impressions that usually end in despair: seasoned, experienced, no junior. Nostalgia doesn't exist, because it is caught and enjoyed as the first cause. Memories metamorphose into incident and sensation. I have studied exotic self-help techniques along with the crude and sometimes amoral ones you are familiar with. From my studies I have amassed the skills needed to invent hundreds more.

Rejuvenated sight expands into the room, to touch the things as a child you could touch. The quickness of muscle follows commands, stretching, allowing yourself to explore. The dried shell crack off piece by piece, each month it cracks off some more. I poured the liquid substance on; it dried while I was in hell. Now I'm not, I can explore.

Walking along a crowded street, I walk it like a treey wood. Or laying in sand absorbing heat -- it's my muscles that resume command.

There was this old man who use to say to me, "I'm glad that everything isn't perfect, think of how boring it would be if everything was perfect." I used to say to him, "No way, man. How would we know anyway?

We have no way of knowing what it would be like if everything was perfect!" Meanwhile, a day drags on and we asked, but again we were left to improvise. Seasons change and that's the problem: I'll be happy tomorrow, but I wish not so I could stop the clock and continue in ascetics, until I get an answer.

I am so sick of the patterns of choice that we fall into, planned by an unknown generation, thousands of generations before even our last names were contrived. The Earth is in need of several non-political revolutions that will make older movements seem so damn naive.

Delusion intrusion, upon a clear and shining day. A clear slate once again dipped into the cauldron containing the stew of the holy war. The amniotic sac of the salvation in Jesus Christ was burst open by the weapons of intellectual despair. The frustration is almost too intense to write a poem. I stay on the fireball; I stay on the glacier. This is not as planned. I am living my enemy's life. I have died a million minutes all. What is this homesickness?

Today, I felt like a failure as I saw you. Big, fresh and manufactured by millions, for you. I felt my mistakes, still adhered to my legs and face; I saw sin clear as day, over and out I'll never say. I also had hope today. Is dualism my only way?

I lose myself in another's perfection. Yet what is there is just like all other pretense. The biggest turkeys are the ones that won't admit that sometimes they too are turkeys. What is all this concern about impressing total strangers? Mutually misguided egotism. The ways of the ego-feeds and ego bleeds.

Sick of the thinking in my head. In my head there is an enemy of my soul, who seeks to see if I'm good looking -- he's at it five or six times a day. Or, whenever a famous hero of mine comes to mind, he compares me with them!

While it lasts it's painful, is it inevitable as the spring in the fall? There is something that we can enjoy in it; a new constitution.

--10--

Gurgling burgling torrent of "Kill, Kill, Kill" vibrates the loveliest teacher, who is out to feast on the recluse beach boy art-teen.

Stifle! Compare! Criticize form over content -- not even that good, processed in a different way.

"--Fashion in literature will destroy us all eventually, when we give in our fruitless rebellion--"

Huh?

"Oh, I was that way, too."

If you were this way, you'd still be this way. There is no turning back.

Why is it that all they can say is "was" -- we don't need it, and we're not running. (The logical linear progression scares the hell out of me). As sure as the day that we die, most will compromise just to appease some maestro mannequin, because we can't even take thirteen seconds of its immobile stare.

"Gee, I'm glad you like it now..."

Art is valid, but some constantly try to shove it in their small mold. They only want to shave edges off it, until it "resembles something."

When I was a teenager I had an idea of what was cool. This color of cool applied to music, art, philosophy, girls, and just about everything else. When things were cool, they convulsed and glowed. Now I witness much of the cool leave me. Sometimes it seems so, but the battle is still on. What would be something I could do that would be totally cool? This would require planning. But would it be cool? Seems our ideas change. But my idea of cool has gotten a little bit commonplace, and thus embarrassing. For instance, eating is now cool, when before it was only a necessity.

Seeing this, perhaps one might say, "I believe you've hooked onto a counterfeit, because the real thing is much more refined, and more difficult to come by."

My peers' life-blood-youth-hope is destroyed in the most mediocre of schools in the guinea pig society of the first television generations. Most of my peers believe that conformity in existing non-conformities is the only other consolation they could seek. They can not recognize those who have not conformed to either.

My repression ends when I see those who don't mean a thing to the Cause. I could rattle off and denounce their patron saints and they'd gasp, punch, or shout. Why must I be faced with their non-option of the linear progression of their forms of "intelligent" "rebellion" against that which stagnates the soul? Why am I finding so few, and so alone? Why do I want to believe that the Earth is only a lower sphere of existence, a training ground, so we will one day be able to hold our own weight in a higher sphere?

Yes, the child poetry can not be faked at your age. It is marked by a day that's real, never able to be cultivated. A diploma won't employ; it takes more than words to appreciate. We now know it takes a physical posturing of the body and neck and most of all facial expressions. Glares, stares, winces, squints, and more stares. A mouth gaping open. Tongues lying flat in the mouth. This physical aspect of the aesthetic is what you're missing. But it is mandatory. But, it is something you must do in your secret closet.

To be the ones who abolish in ourselves the lusts of contemporaneousness and the obsessions with food, and the historical gene pool that they are. We look not only through the eyes of the journalists of the magazine. Meta-history. Meta-critical. We are our lifetime of the whole world. We store all information even if one fact is not known. We are aware of human nature, of what we can still call original sin. When we think about a novelist we look at him as he/she stands as a philosopher. Who needs the documentation of these novelists?

And the reason to not think along certain lines is for me both to obey religion and to sacrifice -- to pay for it. Have I truly given up what I repented of? What have I repented of? I will tell you, I have repented of an endless irresponsible imagination. I have given up my deluded sequences of reverie, the ability to just say anything. Some think they will find convulsive beauty by opening all the doors without preference.

I am standing on a foundation, obviously. By sacrifice we do gain. It is a fact that the unwise really hate. Hating facts is not the way to go.

"Experience in intelligence gives us stored superiority," you say. Am I a trader or just an impostor? Did I get aesthetic experiences only beginning at age nine or have I never come out of my luscious childhood blur? And the bottom line is that many who are first shall be last, and many, who are last shall be first. Did we forget that somewhere along the line?

Cheating whatever it is that keeps information at this low level, we bursted and pounded the posh strawberry textures to hell-metal. Spilling in effervescent crystal abrasiveness, acidic liquid currents the unknown. The result of all this labor is a new type of plasma, which connects our lives in a cerebral haze, a storehouse of says and loves. The ego-scores hinder the trolley car and aerial bus. We weep together, for those moments we are educated by the forgotten.

Observing a dull moment, a jumping joy song, or a one thousand-kilogram sad song, dulled and dampened by being wrapped in soft thick cloth. Out of serious incorporation phase, fecund lips lick mine. My lady wakes up the watery blue, black walled, elegant bathtub.

--11--

That feeling I get, when existence cries out, "The Universe exists, now isn't that weird?"

Thinking of what the world would be like if I weren't born, I realize that the world would not exist to me. Then I question, "Well, the world would go on, but what would the world go on doing?" What is it that the world does and why does it do it? Is it possible that the world could stop doing what it does and, with all the living aboard, start doing something totally different? And how much of All-There-Is is being done by the world: Who makes the world do what it does, or who made the world do what it does? What is the world for except a place that we have our existence in? Is the world aware of us living inside of it? What in the world is going to happen to the world in fifty billion years from now? (Just as every civilization's skyscrapers fall, I can't believe that ours will be inhabited forever).

Why does the world seem like it was set up by someone? Does God exist? And why doesn't this intelligence come down and have coffee with us sometime, and tell us what in the world is going on?

The leveling of humanity. All six month old infants. We are equals. We are amorphous. Presidents, popes, geniuses, psychotics. Before in the mold, the liquids dry, before society paints on its paint from the palette of pain. The current whole mess seems funny, sad, accidental; incongruous with some sort of scripture. Enjoyment is the plasma that is weighed by each and all as the ultimate currency, denoting the might of our nakedness. Reality is that which is going on and on and on and on and on and on, regardless of our opinions of it. Some say reality has yet to kick mankind in the face.

Screaming at the reality of the universe, I start to ask questions: "What else do you do besides set up food chains?" Philosophers, artists and monks, we better start doing it right. Our souls did not have to be born human. We did not have to be born on earth. We did not have to be born on a planet.

The life you gave me, God, I like it a lot. I like the possibilities it implies. I want to go beyond these human limitations of earth someday. I want to break genetic code completely, dissolving neural bonding of our mental limitations. If my eternity doesn't exist, I don't know what I'll do. Speak to the earth, God.... of the ends of sins of man. Are any of us approaching static sainthood? Why are we so judged by the apple of evil and good?

This existence that we are now doing on earth, above land, in respective countries, eating food, drinking liquids, having children, being brainwashed, hiding our eyes from dawn and dusk. What is it that floats out in space -- that muscle beating inside, muscles on the surface beating under the white clouds? It floats around in space and it doesn't look like it is going to go away for at least a few billion years.

Is convincing ourselves on whatever-it-is-we-so-arbitrarily-choose the only way to arrive at the ultimate truth?

When I leave this world, I hope I will look back

with a sanctioned, relieved look, knowing that something better is on the way. Many seek to devour such preparedness for death with a gift of weakness. I had tried to prove that virtue was the meaning for the world's existence. I still sustain a philosophical optimism based on a benevolent God.

If not one human has stumbled upon the truth already, then how can anyone think that a newcomer can bring anything of any importance to philosophy? And even if one did, how would we know which one? The advent of new technologies can perhaps enlarge our knowledge of the universe. Perhaps we can see the cast line at the edge of the universe, and be able to figure out something from that.

The realization that absolute truth has either been found, or not, is where academic philosophy should rest a while and do its considering. It is very good that new blood comes in and takes over from the exhaustion of the old. We need not new versions of the old, but instead an examination of the original problem.

As I remember it, the problem was:

How is it that humanity is on Earth, with animal life and plant life, and how is it that there is no connection between God and large groups of men so that proof of the existence of God would be unnecessary, and his communication to us would be therefore universally accepted? The position that humanity finds itself in is frightening in some ways: why do so many say there are there no answers to their questions when they ask them?

There is the general answer of common sense. It

states that a wise God created the Earth in such a way that the humans who are kind and understanding of their own volition will be rewarded for their virtue. With this answer we can also say that only by a relationship with this God on Earth can people assimilate virtue into their being. Answers to questions posed to God are given but only after a human learns from their experience in how to listen for them.

Thus, the question is incorrect in part. God answers humanity's questions but not to large groups of humans, and no proof of the answers is allowed to survive for others to witness. The meaning of this outcome is such that it is too meaningful for one to experience in a group, the personal experience is needed to understand the answer. Our questions may be answered in different ways such as dreams, conversations, street signs; a divination of the occurrences of one's daily existence.

Is there another way to look at this whole problem? Is it a different problem all together? Are there few similarities in our Earth below and what there is further out in the universe? Does the universe have a big hall of mirrors set up so we can only see what we want to see: the Christian will feel Christ inside his heart, the Buddhist will experience enlightenment, and so on? And after Earth life is over the big hall of mirrors is still there forever; the Muslims go to Allah's heaven and the Buddhists go to Nirvana, and so on.

Some answers tend to annihilate the concept of dealing with a friendly God. If they are taken in a certain direction, these are blasphemies against the Holy

Spirit; the sin of despair. Of course, some of these answers are very lightweight and are arrived at by people who can not emotionally consider a Huge Intelligence that we call God. None the less, if the concept of hope is not included in these philosophies they would be a form of blasphemy against the Holy Spirit -- unforgivable by way of the determination of the subjects.

Food chains of the true aesthetic love, early genius death or physical fitness? I don't like solitude, I just want to join with the King. To be in that country and forever; I will pay their taxes. Hating the limitations that men have to offer, I don't dare to be by myself, isolation is not desired.

What is the God doing so far away from me? Jesus Christ, I want you to shout the truth at me in a vision so that I will finally understand!

You could materialize shoes for the naked children's corroding feet. You could open up a life of beauty for those who so plainly don't have one. You could bring joy to the heart of the sincere philosophers. You could erase the tears of the broken. And You do, yet only when we allow yourself to do it through us.

Over a diseased plateau, desperate words of "No!" -- do they seem to get a "so"?

God helps and heals. All these hundreds of diseases, aneurysms, genetic syndromes, and other conditions. Are we motivated for the cause of a cure?

"We are the cattle withheld in fences, we are the chickens brought up in cages. In a world where all good myth receives praise, let our fullest fun blaze."

Waste the destructive scheme planned by those much larger than ourselves. Fry or cremate the gelatinous strands that short circuit our lives. I hope to not quench the dream of hope to look into the illusively consoling face of pessimism. Born in a world with few doors out, our bodies get old and we die. Few miracles trespass the laws of nature; do the laws of nature seem to trespass the miracle of our existence?

Don't fret, one day we will know all things: all things in consciousness, or all things in the death of soul.

In some sort of strange corner of the dimensions of various things known to us as the Universe, a chamber exists where various beings go about their business. A biochemical oddity among oddities; softened primates, their evolution caused by fear. Some strange lighting falls upon this corner of the dimensions of various things known to us as the universe. A bread and cheese and wine cafe. Some quaint functions of being. Some macrocosmic dime store -- there is even optimism in this!

Looking up at the moon through a window, I was lying on my back in an enclosed porch-like room. The dark, purplish clouds were lit up around the bright round moon. I admired the distance from the earth to the moon. I thought: I know there is more life in the universe than just this planet. Life is benevolent to our souls...if we are a little lucky. Does luck, blind random chance, have everything to do with it? Would God give birth to some with mental retardation, and I know that's not the worse one can have; a soul is a soul...but there are some that are more miserable, and there is no doubt in anyone's mind. Sometimes, if they are able, not even their's. Well, it's not fair. Is it luck? Karma?

Most of what we try to pin on God is myth; old fables that have nothing to do with what the truth is of such matters. We have our standard blasphemies.

Is the documentation of the thousand millions, in Earth time's progeny, kept in the eyes of the current generations?

--12--

Science can be a fool's religion; paupers in the love of now. Forever remember the simple sorrow, but emotional levels read nil. Because of all in said and softly, whispers a toxic chemoblast. Forever remember we don't own the Earth; scientist, you hold the vein. Vein open upon the body, the planet spreads her yielding juice. Vault over the fence. Spring over your bounds: pity it is that so many of your kind hate religion. You can't believe in God, no, not if He's not you somehow.

As intelligence dwindles, atheism grows. The reason thereof is the mind's rationalization of its insecurity's hyperactivity in ratio with the possibility and inclination of the mind to ponder the abstract. The abstract they ponder is not the real abstract, even if it was, it gets interrupted and put down every ten minutes -- the linear progressions are not made. The mundane in insane has become growable in classrooms. And Satan scars the really good people into thinking they will be the Anti-Christ someday.

I am an eternal indestructible, did you remember you were too? A tree of thistles does not bring forth fruit of grapes. On and on. Falling off like shadows go the hurting dogmas. Which ones...it's hard to say.

"Speak up atheist, let's see those answers, or at least reasons for your glorified agnosticism. I see, I must suffer the pain of asking more specific questions. Is your decision beyond trend? Is your life a dream that doesn't count? Is this next death the only death? What is death?

Granted that each soul is equally born on earth with no established answers, but are the answers here?"

"Being just a human, no one can tell you anything of the highest value."

Being a human has nothing to do with it.

Still, the slow sheet of water descends upon us. We ask only forgiveness as we soak in the pond.

Sustentation, removing the guilt; turning to gold, cracking the hilt.

Big bad killing philosophies, erased the need for human hope, concerning the things that need to be explained to us. Do we have the possibility of understanding abstract mechanisms of function, or higher larger vessels of living? Some think there may be no understandable God images, only more parts to the whole; parts that are more elaborate than our part. And the part they play is more important to the unseen. Are our eyes able to see; can a neuron be told about the whole human? Big bad killing philosophies, clouding the concerning about things that need to be explained to us.

Now seeing Freud's fruits swell in the sanctified land, and as they are distributed, eaten and digested it is conceivable to imagine that the end is now at hand. To some things, I want a closed mind, for too often straight and narrow is the way. Blind hedonism is to wait too long for something you can't have.

The smiles are deceitful; an open house, an open invitation. They put out the bait, and set the trap. A hungry yearning for more fuel, more fuel for the ego. They want a crown, but seem to deserve a grave. And they tell me there is no difference between good or bad, but they never show me the fruits of their higher evolvement.

The Hedonist, it draws a jab at them Simpletons, the damage it does gives it a lift. Judged wise by its peers in its ability to despise. Does slander come easy everyday?

"Anti-man are we, here we see, limitations in thought abounding."

Psychological debris drainage system. Their end product has become decrepit. This is what has become of their ideas. Yet, they started out with such good intentions.

Preposterous! -- the definition of these things, yet given in such plainness of acceptability. Will you accept and be accepted? Will you deny and be forgiven?

To analyze the motivation for the cause according to crude and banal psychology, would be to further tighten your eyelids until your very eyeballs are squashed like grapes in a little boy's fingers.

Can you see still? Absolutes are absolutes. The only absolutes we can be sure about are absolute questions. Mighty eternal questions which can never be rationalized away, because their answers do exist.

Now at the mood to write a poem, I snarl at the injustice around me. Another noble loser, another Franz Kafka. The vanity of the pathetic envelopes me. So I see all this and I become free. Not another human monument to the depths of despair. The Noble Loser muse flees from me.

But some are not so lucky. The Opener-Table grants them free admission, and they rejoice at this, their first recognition. The treatment is steady and long. The release of their bats produces contamination. Although they release the bat thoughts thinking, "Key to Free," with the release comes the gradual bits of death and the smiles now stink. This contamination comes from the bats which carbuncle several small dwellings in their once pure smile.

But wait! Not with New Books! Books that will eventually grant them friends. The Opener-Table will provide new books for them. But still, too many second looks, too many reconsiderations. The Opener-Table opens their mind so the bat thoughts can fly out and return to them to land in dwellings in their once pure smile.

The scope of this negative system is not as real, as the Lies from the Pit seem it all to be. The conclusions are results from pollutions of evidence; the logic employed is thus denied its chance. The facts are twisted then bloated into volumes of the historical novels they write with the ink they have extracted from the fears of the masses -- who only want to believe in something so badly.

In the way they laugh... many birds of uncommon plumage flew into corrosive sheets. In the way that they laugh... many who are earnest still work hard for their food.

The outcome is despair, confusion, frustration, insanity. The Lies from the Pit have gotten their desired results. But the escape was made well known, from the beginning we were shown. But, we misunderstood the work of it. The blind spotted vanity of the intelligentsia has sadly captured its own into a thought-style without a solid home. Every night their dream machine tells them: "Our end product has become decrepit. We resisted societal good and that changed us. We are sad and rotten. And that is the fruit of our labors."

Another enemy of the people, we the people; no critics praise his warmth. Enemy in subtle instances; the essence though is all too obvious. He is the new superstar of the art world. His name is shown to us with the barrel of their gun aimed on us, "this is art, do you really *understand* it?" A new, subtle form of robbery.

We will like what we are shown eventually.

All there is in the universe is shown to us in only what we remember. Some humans choose what most of humanity is shown. It is therefore up to us to get in there and reveal more information and vision.

--13--

The masculinity and the relaxation of the facial muscles, with the ease of leisure and the eloquence of cash, encases the luxuries, in swirls and scarves, and drapery. Entomb the frontal region. Rest in peace.

Craftsmanship: the eximious, the invaluable, the exorbitant, priceless, unconscionable. The skill of sweat jewel-cutters drip. Schooling in sequence from age two to twenty-five -- check one. Proper attitude learned-- check two. Original technique of manipulation of medium -- check three.

As they fasten the buckles in warm, painted, clothed, embellished rooms there is never contact with the millions more. As the maid, butler, and cook work to prepare the house for the pleasure of the family and guests, they are all enclosed, lucky to be away from the outside, where many humans are enclosed in a forest, outside in the elements, untamed, straggling in clothes made of such a coarse and a simple design.

While the husband and wife live a life of fulfillment of will and wealth, in houses that sparkle, the motions of the masses goes on outside their door. If contact is made, contamination of a sort occurs undoubtedly on both parts.

"Behold the Spirit!"

The phrase is uttered to both worlds and each feel at home with it.

The vain coach travels down Shadybrook Lane in the fall. Landscapes are ignored, non-family members are deplored. Those who don't fit into the trend are harmless. Those who do fit into the trend are watched carefully. Do they fit in above or below? -- the essence of the show.

"So this where I'm so posed to be, in with the models, well done hair. The youth and the beauty. Perfection in appearance . . . it's so well done."

"So this is where I'm so posed to fit in. In with the girls in red and green dresses. Such good young ladies; this must be perfection."

"So this is where I'm so posed to fit in, the style council, wealthy poems of waters, the airs of rustic autumns with maple leaves on the ground and in the sky."

The soft breezes, the fitting ground, to the model's land -- the Fashion Show!

"The thing about the rich is that they have been allowed to grow by doing; allowed to do by having money. Money brings with it respect. Respect puts a person in the spotlight, allows them to make decisions, exercising their minds. People think with their status and their abilities increase the more they act. Someone who doesn't make large decisions often, nor who can act spontaneously at will, may feel and act less intelligent than one who does all those things."

The airport is like home to the prepared in overnight luggage loads and the assurances that the rest is on its way.

"The plane will take us to Egypt, once there, there will be tables and fine cigarettes and cups of coffee."

"The will: necessary actions and lifelong desires;

fulfillment, enjoyment progression. Will: the power to be actualized. Will; the right decisions, some sweet steady course. The first steps are in the home. Enough work already present. A home: an environment to work in. A job: the only way to get money, the pieces of your life if you work too hard and unhappily to get it."

A man should work. The work he does should provide him the power he needs to get his real work done: his own enjoyment; some fulfillment of his own will. Life has not considered many artist's art to be work.

Why? Why are they penniless? When they give and give and give of themselves on the pages and the tapes which are all they can afford to buy.

What about that line: "the rich were good in the last life"? If years of asceticism will be wasted in reckless pleasures of the next life of rewards on earth, then what occurs in the life after that?

What one misses in religious observation is impossible to gain in monetary expenditures and intercontinental ventures. The similarities in essences are many, but the frontal regions are only cultivated by religious devotions resulting in sincere losses. The last shall be first. The lost shall last.

Those creeks with black mud, and branches with bright birds, see the life that the universe sets free for those who can't afford to live in big cities. The birds have better ears; their minds are shaped by the way they hear. Their entire physical form is shaped by their constant thought.

However one opens their eyes, hurricanes can be friendly still.

"Sorry, I made little money. Sorry, I will never walk those amber deserts with you. Sorry, I have to live my life in a relative silence. It's funny: I'm sorry for the popular way, although it's not my fault."

The Earth is just a strange place, so much for us to say, to catch up for our own misguided criticisms of the status quo or the innocent stranger.

Do you see what you have been doing, sneering in all faces, bland and cute? You still seek what you have, and you'll never find what you're slowly losing.

Can't you see your folly, human? Do you really think you can sustain the good?

Some may look at your life, looking at the things that you like to do, and the things that you have achieved and they will see enjoyment, they see the grass greener. Whoever you are, if you need a few kind words, listen to me and enjoy the things of yourself that they see. Enjoy it in a different way than you have known. Enjoy your life the way they have seen it.

Zero mobility, how did it get to be this way? You and I, and those prisoners to a parent's house or studio apartment. Others talk about farms feeling like a long lost friend. Some enjoy a leisurely plane ticket on alternate months. I guess there is a lesson to be learned either way. Hey, it's good to be back home.

Thousands of souls die every day, with their thousands of thoughts that had been thought. These thoughts -- much of them must have been so much the same!

Each soul cared for so much -- and so many who cared so much for them!

"I'll be good looking till I die. For the helpless and suffering, I'll be with them and we shall together cry. Money goes in my hand to buy my escape into an un-populated land. Sell my soul for a few years, provide the earth with the proper tears."

The breeding ground's ground is getting harder, the thin green stem's thread white roots try to dig in. The lusts of this world are the devices to make us unable to live in our Father's Home.

Can we see that God creates us to be what we always wanted to be? If He didn't, than that would be a mistake in design.

-14-

Exercises in pragmatic afters. Recluse from the winds of change. Mono-unified in primordial sequence sustaining colossal chords of the ingredients of the planet. No concept of what it is like all at once, I take three steps back. Yellow winds with black white shadowing and showering and I'm warm. The rent is paid for all this month. Searching for the words that will turn on us, religious experiences should somehow be mandatorily desired.

Most final products are in a constant flux. How come I feel like this -- like it is so old? How come I feel it and it's like my own set of colors, but they are everyone's everywhere's colors? It is not Surrealism, it's not e.e. cummings, it's not even my favorite rock bands. Is it to be gotten from a perfect recollection of childhood attitudes and experiences?

I want to stay here in touch with a me that was almost gone. I have managed to rescue it from the rambunctious wasteland of my peers as artists, poets, composers -- the dramatic effect is all I intend by this statement.

They will get nowhere without that which is of the Spirit.

Machine invented which unites our hope into a constant issuing out, a constant presence emitted from its blower into our living rooms: "I am so glad I got this thing! Now I'll never need memory again! Good bye Nostalgia. Hello Yesterdays!"

No, it is not quite that easy. And I know what its

like. We are selling our souls for pretty cheap prices.

"I'm looking at my body, to see if it's sexy. Undesirable worries. Strain. Tension. Despair. There is much trouble and I know what it is like."

The enjoyment of life is not a matter of status; the vanity of labor does not equal success. Plan ahead. Take a Rest.

We can all do things in the future if we pay the price of time and patience, in every aspect of our lives today. Salvation; saving.

Everything was set up to work just right. Everything would have been so beautiful. But, instead we bit the apple of comparison. If there is a progression in virtue like there has been a progression in science, then the future will smell like roses, tulips, cherry, apple, peach, and pear blossoms and daffodils, and like all the rest, including the rare ones too, like the African and Middle Eastern flowers, some of which are presently extinct.

Let's throw science on the back burner for a while and concentrate on a progress in ethics.

The strongest fastest rate of vibrations, the initial impulse -- watch for distractions which act to weaken the vibrations. The idea must be kept strong; vibrating in its original state. There is so much time. I see the years, the hours of the day go by like a sandy beach. There are so many chances. So many hours to metaphorically paint one's metaphorical canvas.

Humans feel and compose edifying looks of emotional feelthoughts. A planet as a You or Me spins around the Sun, spins around the Galaxy, spins around the Center of the Universe as we know it. What do we know about it? How little! Anyway, extensions are present in my plan as seeing something more than meets the lie(brary).

If we had a brain the size of a Saint Bernard dog, do you think we would think the way we do now? If we had a heart the size of a Jesus Christ, do you think we'd feel the nice things more? The moral lessons a man has learned, map a true progress. They are firm steps, such as not to use intimidation on people.

The mandatories are so silent: tomorrow, life, deeds, death. How much pain, much pleasure? Will I smile with God, or try to reach the surface of the fade? The fade that may be immortal organic death.

A billion glories may be yesterdays one day. Right now I'm safe. I've always been so, but will it be all I'll ever know? What a grand loving scheme. Love is so beautiful.

Today is so beautiful. I love today. Love and biology, science and trust, ice and energy, depth and bliss. All I know now is safety. The mandatories are so silent.

See my vision: a million negatives will give us the one positive worthwhile. I believe in being awake, some are asleep, some are awake, I'll fess up to this one. But, in being addicted to self-help, an objective philosophy, theology, or just any answers to the bigger questions, do not enter in at all. Some forms of considered enlightenment are too subjective.

--15--

When war is here. When war is here. If time doesn't end, and there are people after we die. If the Earth has an end, but the concept of being can not die.

"I would surely do this, I would be a part of a foundation, a stepping stone, if I was a part in a sequence, a sacrifice in a line I knew would succeed, I would do it, I'd be a sacrifice with others. That would do, a link in a chain, a piece of the puzzle, if it would succeed; I would be part of that foundation."

He had a delusion. He thought that like the chemical processes in a cell, like the energy needed for a solar system orbiting around the center of the galaxy, like the energy of planets around the sun, he was on Earth to trigger the impulses of rotation, to "apocalypse" the end of a stage, to keep the ball rolling.

"Worthless anti-government screams only to realize this too shall end. Only with you friend do I exist; I need you more than you think."

"Too many people for the jocks to be so selfish. I can't believe in the survival of the fittest. That's where religion comes in. That and the only single answers to whatever the questions are."

Remind yourself, political vain ambition, archangelic, yet evidence that Satan is at it again. The again is now, but who sees it as such? The vain lonely country is resurfacing -- move out of fascist homestead. No matter the respect, the paternal instincts destroy the child instincts.

Do we have a constant, that is, will there always be for us the them that are arrogant and dishonest, who aim to intimidate. The them that are so far from us in deed? We are equally their them?

In what direction do their missiles fly? Surely towards themselves -- and this is also metaphorical. Complete protection is impossible when you're on the offense (What a paradox!). Bullets cracking, bombs exploding, pain imploding, lives slowly leaving. For this their missiles fly. (And this is also metaphorical).

Why do they build the guns? Only for one purpose: to pierce the skin of man and beast, with a demon of hot metal.

Why the dichotomy of politician and artist? Why the power structure in the glorified playground of the world that is our politics? Holiness is for the gentle. Holiness is for the small.

There is silence in North America. There is silence in Europe. There is still silence in war-torn areas. Run away games they should play when they are seething in their hating games. In the U.S.A and elsewhere, there are groups of people who volunteer their time to various organizations that collect donated items from the public and use these donated items for therapy in alcohol detoxification programs. In America, there are also groups of people, politicians who are cloaked in the pretensions of working for the good of humanity. These, clothed in their assumption, perhaps pass by these Salvation Army, or St. Vincent de Paul, volunteers on the street, and snicker inside about the type of person this is, who looks just like their mother.

There is a type of mental illness that causes its human host to rise to some type of political power, or influence, in the host's country and coerce the forces that be to start a war, or accept a foreign country's actions as war worthy. Most good common folk think of war as the last thing that anyone would want, but there is this mental illness, which can have its effect in variable degrees. It is the illness of turning the trick from times of peace to big time belligerence.

The insane one who is infected with the disease may be powerful enough to get his sickly dream fulfilled. Throughout history we have seen the war-hungry come into power -- their play.

Mucky higher in common, sweaty rich deserve the best. Toddler elite in understanding, sharper than even some real people I know.

Popularis, not so mutant now, there are possibilities in the one, two, three. Might as well shoot up for the stars, maybe all the way up is where I'll be. "In all honesty, it would be easy for me too, not so much as a sell out, but a noise." But do it evenly and do it quick. Ask in prayer and do it quick. Go from here to there, in more steps than three.

"Forget commercialism, we have got the message now. We have just got to tell you, there is nothing violent that we will do. And you know we are not fascist. So why don't you listen?"

Not enough barking from the pit, not enough at least at the right moments. You enchant the healers and they heal themselves. No one there knows this. So polish your furniture or take a warm bath, but don't judge yourself today please. For, I am here reading in this room, and I don't want you to start our nausea.

The only way to escape the futility of the machine and the redundancy of it in and on our lives is to ignore it, without, or as if, being naive. I could word paint phrases of blues and oranges, festive organic architectures and in combinations of life and tool, but what if we lost our souls? We must be warned. Warned against lies from the East and materialism of the West. We must prove with useful logic. As with every writing down in quick indignation, the happy saved get happily turned off. What is the end product of all our problems? Seems to me to be the worst excuse for the day. Sure, I've felt that anger, too, though I realize that what we want to be, or hold on to, is what's left. Hold us in our arms and speak slow words of obvious truth. Achievements of love are always in the past, I'm happy to repeat myself on this point. Our hearts are sealed in the hope of resurrections. Our achievements are our yesterdays' efforts.

Why does our advice to others fall as worthless trash before our feet, when we try to apply it to ourselves? Can we ever catch up to the love lost by ourselves that was meant to love others? Lovelessness is a habit that many with true love have unfortunately acquired.

When one sees the world's pain, there seems a lot for one to say; to slip off into advice, and end that way. You have turned around these things and said to, "Break off! recoil -- I've not been through all the soil!" It seems bad to me too. Dishing out the plans was always this easy; all future and no today. One day: the day that common sense came to the earth. Everything we knew to do that was right was done. We had a minor, but meaningful, redistribution of wealth. We had a laugh on the town's privates. We dismantled the bombs. We lived in the churches. We did what everyone knows is right.

Will the happy day come upon the human race? A day when all love is revealed to humanity? All purpose shown, all comfort grown upon aching, hurting humanity? Searching, we are left dumb by a greedy, manipulative machine. Kept stupid because stupid people don't ask questions; they don't revolt against a stupid landscape.

Common sense: the precious refined liquor of the nonexistent noble classes who will seldom offer a gulp to the modern Earth's generations. The day common sense came to the Earth's populations, reversing the decompositions of the prayer's recompense, which was seen that the prayers were said. But will the happy day show up? Maybe it will, individually in each of our lives' end. Perhaps we will be given our pay. How optimistic!

--16--

Four walls and a ceiling and floor that have nothing to do with the plan of this room. Outdoors by way of all the brain cells: their memories beating in pulses at once. Only good things are seen somehow. Goes to show we learn from experience. To be enclosed in the roominess of virtue and to never leave, my sinful nature dissolves -- that is the magic, that is the alchemy. The alchemy is to be a lover of humanity; to wash our brother's feet.

Pulse beat throb continues all our representation. Yet, of course, only what we have been shown now beats in this fullest. (With that statement you have the mechanism of hope). You're in this room, not now as you now read, but in a time somewhere. Go home and think about it. Home of brain cells scan whole soul's life forever. Yet, I didn't say when those brain cells scat, you'd be out of a you-know-what. God helps and heals, but only as you burst out of your forehead and cry for help.

In the outside world Madam/Sir, the universe is depraved and loveless, or, is it just the fresco inside your dome? Let's just say culture has lied and you have bought the old lie of Egypt, Rome, China, India, Babylon, and Sodom. There are only two places, to be in the Room of Virtue or not.

Oh Heavenly Father, there are so many philosophical liars down here; wolves in wolves' clothing. They are here to rip the sheep apart, by something that resembles a sickly cannibalism. This is a nightmare immensely. Yet, a nightmare in real life is such a tragedy. Even the word "tragedy" is not strong enough.

"Lord, make me to have love double what I now have for others. The neighbors have to work harder for their food, and many kill what's best in their souls just to keep their jobs -- how long will this go on? Forever? Thank you, Lord, for in this revelation there is love found doubled."

Dear would-be poet, herein lies the map of the true quantity of poetry, indistinguishable to ordinary eyes. It is the death and smearing of our life, or not so right now, that must stain your page. But first, you must remember, it is mandatory to be a sage. (We are all a sage, if only on the back of our faces). Poetry is your glory, yet the true quality of poetry is the death and smearing of our life, or not so right now, or not so forever.

"As we sat back on the sofa, my muse and I chatted. She was reassuring me so gently. It was so good."

"Yes, you did your work down there"

"I'm so glad it is over. It can be very scary yet extremely dull down there."

"But we accomplished our mission. We were the philosophical-poet-artist. We furthered intelligence down there."

"The security of being here is great. You know, I had forgotten the truth of immortality. They have you worry there like a sad dog -- a mere sixty or seventy spins around a star."

"Yes, but some of that's been changed now."

"Oh yeah, but truly so little. The demonic powers are too intense where I was."

"Yeah, but just think: we can relax in the heavenlies; for all time we are free. There is no end to our world. By the creativity of millions like us we will be entertained and edified."

"Art down there is so often hideous."

"But that's all over. Relax"

We were young and children and I probably knew then that remembering the good of the past is a way of creating the good of the future, or the present. Yes, this is the key that I've been waiting for. We have all been going about furthering insanity in the right way all this time. If you can eat this aesthetic answer, then trust it, and even though your past contains nightmares, don't worry, for sooner or later you'll realize that you are the only tool for you, and you'll happily accept the past's items. Soon, you'll be remembering the present time's todays as certain as you'll be remembering yesterdays. This makes for a happy future. Thus, being born again is real in many ways. The Lord will take us in His hands; we are not just playing alone down here.

The happy cry emits its sad virtue in our lives when the glorious overwhelms through. A nice way to integrate oneself in reality.

--17--

Illuminated ashen staircase, arm outstretched to you, pulling you upward, where is sporadic quivering twilight. It feels like soft hyperventilation. The arm pulls you into a loft where there is sedated stillness that indeed lasts as long as you want, until finally, weeks later, you feel restless...

This peace is from God, there is his trademark all over it. There is the success of your spouse waiting there. With your spouse your life is fulfillment: you're not anti-social; you have love; you are a beautiful human being: you've matured into a sensitive adult.

Explosion of commitment. Running around particles of introspective murmurings. I want to articulate but don't have the chance. I forge ahead, I alone -- isolated evolution.

"Let's have no more compromise brothers, sisters. Let's die once and for all to the gossip behind our backs!"

What do I find? I am faced with compromise. Compromise can kill constantly in degrees. Degrees of ever increasing disease. Disease weans upon sin's crusts covering the victims of the promise of quenching ego.

Even if I don't fully understand the heaven of any religion (whether being in a city for a million trillion non-years, or being in the House of God the same), I won't be too quick to invent my own conception of it. Of course, all descriptions of heaven are probably allegorical.

"Eye has not seen, nor has ear heard, nor has entered into the hearts of man, the things that God has planned for those that love Him."

Further new modal sentience: the light in taste and feel, is only example one of how we like a meal.

The amorphous joy of the heavens is what we expect, don't be sad if you don't know it yet. There is not one among us who has been there, or so I suspect. In our future childhood above the planet, there is something that will be the way it used to be. No sickness, vices, or major crises will bring my life upon the scales. The days past by the way I want them. No second thought for prosperity. What an insurance plan I've hooked onto. I'm the benefactor when the casualty.

We can clear up my case. It will take effort though, for complete repentance and then a cleansing from the Above. I now have almost drowned, but You can work it out, now that I need You.

The fields and plants grown from the seeds that I have sown are despair for me, clouds for me, torment for me. What can I be in You, where is my way? Whenever I get up to walk, my habits are my path. It must seem too hard to stop on the road to hell.

I keep forgetting about church; I rarely go there anymore. I have never felt bad walking out of any of those services that I went to. The spiritual people there, brothers and sisters, would welcome me, just like they would anyone else, with open arms. Some could provide an example for me and make the transition real, yet painless.

"The curse on man, doled out by Almighty God, is that humans would have to work. The curse on man, placed by mighty Satan, is that it would be hard not to worry. But why create a human to live in misery, uncaring? That's not God. So, if He can't give us the bucks, he must be up to something better? -- Oh, how we shall be in those glorious days. Hyper-even-to-the-point-of-absurdity religious optimism. Blood on the scars that are our dreams. Artificial (although non-fiction) landscapes that bleed on our hopes. The metabiological monster earth consumes. I'll scream because you won't."

The nature of the world as a death factory to many seemed very valid. How and why should consciousness continue after death if it is just preoccupied with greed, slothfulness, malice and pride?

Culture chomping on chances of being a real hero. I live a life that is part of others. My culture is chomping on the way I chose. The way I chose is not the way I'm being. Would Jesus find any heroes today? What's He seeing? Probably what I'm truly being. Culture chomped a whole that's me.

Dropping off layers of dogma and repression, freedom appears as a vacationing morning in a parking lot of a chain motel. Bark on a tree bough trunk going down to the ground in a Northeastern USA park.

Closet marionette, felt edges made in Germany. Airplane travel changes tickets and keys, radiator heating the winter. Inside gifts and tools and supplies, words, paints, keyboards, speakers -- a tie to wear to a premiere. Oh, I won't mention the wars in South America or the starvations in Africa. No, let's talk of our statement and the crowd. We can get back to where we started, but somehow I missed and came here.

"Don't put yourself on the outside."

"Don't stay in the inside."

"Don't stay above."

"Don't sink below."

"Stay where we can see you!"

You have got to do more. You have got to spill it out until there are discoveries up on the sand, out of the dirt, bringing out the hose, or use a wire brush. More than meets your flabby metal detector is in your brain.

It's not OK in your prefab, I prefer one built on rock, the love that we get who love Him, will never stop. It's not so much that you don't believe in God, it's that you don't believe in us. The journey has only taken all this in our lives, every moment that we've awakened to the Outside...to the Outside. The results of the poll are very enchanting, leading to indulgence.

Be careful your exile does not occur from a dream world heaven. Exile from your imagined heavens made your life a life in hell only because your heavens never existed -- only your Hells did. This is not even what I wish to tell you. Are you miserable and do you dream much? It is not because of your dreaming that you suffer. It is a matter of using your dreaming as currency in this world.

Dreams of heaven you must dream now on earth. Our heavenly pleasures planned by another? Plot the colonial maps of attainable mental paradises. A dream is real close to being there. See what boundaries you can fly past on your childhood bicycle. Remember, it's an afternoon during a sticky summer in front of the new houses they are building down the street.

How can I sum things like this together? How can I make it flow better? Maybe things like this should not flow together too smoothly.

--18--

Dear Lord, the meeting we're making, You wanted to have it all along. I love you all the way, You love me more than I can love you. The family down here is a show off, it is not pure in any good eye. To keep hearts young and treaded in the fields of childhood, I hope they've treaded it more recently than what I know of them. The recent is not receding, and the plan of our whole life might be, to remember that still present substance, of what we were like at age three.

I feel you constantly want me to be satisfied. But this is a paradox, a contradiction. I don't like to despair: it makes you sad then. But I can't pretend -- things move too slow. Isn't there anything you're going to do that will be instantaneous? Instead, it seems we will do it weakly, over a period of invisible days or months.

At night when I dream, where are those lands on earth which I created in my dreams? The attics, rustic attics, noble classes attics, have you seen? Only in dreams I am young, only at night I am noble.

What happened to my land: my terrain, the trees, groups of trees, grasses, bramble? Where is my field! Where is the ground and breeze that brought forth the nourishment of my soul? Do I no longer deserve my landscape? Am I a new essence of human, lowered to a new classification: adult? The playgrounds of childhood...further description would only defile the intent. My way back to the past seems purely a financial question, yet this is only a symptom of the problem I've acquired.

Get me out of this urban mess!

Damn battle I won in the heat of the day Everyday; it is so real I can't even scream. Sick of holding in the waste of my life. My progress has been made, but again the damn battle I won in the heat of the day Everyday tries to kill me with its memory. I only have need to remember the stages in the fight I've already fought and won. Higher consciousness is a carrot on a string they think they hold above me. I am a professional, just like they are, but the title "professional" is qualitatively only a figurehead.

Do dogmatics work? Am I a soldier for the esoteric or the exoteric? On the fields of the spiritual search, I've always known how to do the ascetic. To give up art, hate, and some food, in order to charge the battery included with us. Contact with the splendid ubiquities of truth does more than restore this battery's energy; it enables latent energy to spring to life in our being. The truth is a food: come let us feast till eternal fatness is secured! Let's explode our common sense! Let's see that we do know very much.

The higher up you go, the less criminals are to be found. The fields are clearer and you originate more of the sound. The walls are thicker there. There is no restriction to access.

To be alive and happy, breathing in fondest childhood memories. I see I am a man who wants to make a lot of money and own a home. The expansion of sincere truths.

Society of Cheerful Geniuses. To be alive: found the key, found the rhythm, found the tone. There is desire to document. Remembering the future opened by the past. The past frequently looks bright -- it is a useful mechanism that the past frequently looks bright. Be careful about hating your past, because it will give you a chance for hating your present. The universe is opened by the past.

Truth was spread out on the table in front of us. We ate heartily until real reeled. We were then charged and lifted off. What more is there to be said; the truth is a necessary food that refills our real.

If the weather's fine and you got the time, it's your chance to wake up and plan another brand new day...it's a beautiful morning! The Gospel: all chances forever. It wasn't too hard for them to arrange our eternity for us, so they said they would and they did. Eternal life in a corner of the universe. How nice of them to set us up, spinning and on our way. Thirty billion years from now -- I'd be happy to still thank them for it.

The eternal mechanism of consciousness is the eternal noumenal. We can be sure of the fact that if all humanity and all life on earth were to die, some type of conscious being somewhere would still exist. To think the universal and complete extinction of all consciousness could occur is to think the most absurd idea!

Christmas morning multiplied by millions. Were

you the ones who ran down the stairs to get to the tree that morning?

Hypothetical popular, here one evening. I give it the option: to go or no? The solution?... appears. It's boring. The treasure is securely hidden. Stages.

--19--

Like a mechanism of softness, slowly spinning like a rowboat on softest waters. Like an overcoat stretched over the whole domain. It's a feral beast; it grins its teeth, eyes, and claws. Like a tomb symphony when you're in tune with it, like your life's badness when you're not: the Will of Schopenhauer, it's only as good as your brain has cells to think. In Metempsychosis, all is now accounted for: the boy born with only stumps for limbs, the girl born with one eye; the two born as one. Reincarnation, yes, it' s possible -- the answer for difficult questions.

Post, yet still embracing the false peace notion, little more than chemical changes in brain. And it is sad, but way too sad to let go, and the truth is just too simple. (That's why they adhere to a philosophy that questions if it's good to exist). They will never be saved; it would destroy their reputation. What's accepted now in their religion of anthropology will be in rigor mortis tomorrow. And yesterday's true pearls, are hard to recall in their unphotogenic (to say the least!) memories.

There was once a world view where there was no hell, only heavens. We were reincarnated thousands of times, we were loved by a higher love of life. There was no fear of losing salvation necessary in this religion. There was no God, only a Luminescent Cotton Ball at the center of all existence. It might still be this way, but I doubt it. I have seen the silent sorrow, and felt the price and the purchased possession, and it seems to me to be real.

I wanted to go through all my days in a perfumed way with Eastern Religious essential oils. I thought it was the highest, and in vegetarian health, I tried my high pursuit: yogic meditation.

Backtrack into the Global Moon. More than Moon -- Earth, Sun, Galaxy, Tao! I wanted that adept, extremely mobile yogi personality type. I wanted to master all that the yogi's said we could. I must concede, maybe I failed, but who knows. If I failed, I'll have a chance again to assume the asanas and ascend my kundalini and have it burst into a bus ride of the dense nectar safaris. In another lifetime.

Lifetime.

"Bliss is nothing's trademark," I can feel the beauty in that! But it's: "Wake Me Up, Father, Son, and Holy Spirit." Two stories being told at once, two films being shown simultaneously on the same screen. The enormous gulf for most, when you come right up to it; right down to the facts.

To go on feeding one's astral body, with prana and tofu, or to put all those types of more esoteric cares in the One who created me for eternity? In the alchemy of soul department, we must assimilate the proper frequency from decoding messages written in books, but in the Judeo-Christian God's way there is Consciousness working with consciousness.

Do we lead ourselves to not see the evil perpetuated by the Llamas of Tibet but only the Priests of old

Spain? What do the thousands of years of the oppression of class slavery instituted and upheld by the Brahmins mean to you? "Hitler was a vegetarian," so the saying goes. There are no human gods, only those of us with better posture.

Obviously, the idea of reincarnation has much possible "fascism" intrinsic in it. Who are the older souls here among us today, and should they treat others as children and worse? Of course not! Should they set up their rank systems based on birth, genetics, hormones, controlled anger, etc.? Should we bow to them to get only an ecstatic touch on our foreheads?

Oh, why don't we see, if there is anything to see, that which we were not before our conception; at the sexual action. That's scary: if there isn't life before birth there might not be life after death. I don't want it to fade. If there are yogic exercises, I'll do them. If there are sins to avoid and ones to ask forgiveness for, better yet, for I do not wish to be a prisoner of my neural ganglion!

--20--

When Christ is inside you, has He ever cried? These are the most thunderous wet tears one can cry. He isn't crying about you. He is crying about love.

Sorrow, the proper tears all might cry. The happy crying, it's there too. An emotional life? I'd say it would be better. Deep notes with only the top half coming through. Who can live a life all of checks and balances? Cultivated sorrow is an allure for the cause.

"The overreaching Post-Surrealisms are encompassed by virtue. The paintings are accompanied by separate patios. The musics are in conjunction with delicacies."

God is one: faith, sacrifice, answer.

Some forfeit the enigmas for a golden couch of opium. They chose a life of blindness and forsake minor quiet disciplines. They lose the full joy, but gain the minute's mountains.

The mammoth injustice again rears and cries, swiney yet deep, achieves to despise. That we have been wronged, severely and detrimental (to us), yet subconscious and hidden (to us) -- yet, absolutely: it would be forbidden by us.

The Babbling Fool screaming injustice because his inferiors are acting inferior, creating a complex in the Babbling Fool.

"Her voice makes one want to eat food, it destroys the spiritual. I must always now drink coffee. Some things must be sustained."

"I caught you stealing from me to realize that all those years my youth you have siphoned through your plastic straws. Were your acts conscious or subconscious? Your sickly plastic straws of stories, robbing me of my youth, day by day. I've learned -- can I show others? Can I protect exploited youth, fresh minds and souls, can I protect the exploited old, with the knowledge that I've learned?"

"The energies that I have fed you do not seem to do you much good. The fact that you stole them from me in the first place shows something very wrong with you."

"It was frightening to watch the way he enjoyed the simple things in life."

"I had to just say no to you. My fear of freedom is all gone now. I have to turn my back on you. You are truly the chains on my life."

I imagine a soul screaming from its grave, "Oh! If I could only be a consumer!"

The soul screams from its grave, "If only I could have my sunglasses on! If only I could eat cheeseburgers now that I am nervous." The soul screams, and it is the only one. And not alone, its mind is not his. And it wasn't his own for many years before his death.

What is a soul? Something that we are usually born with, but usually don't die with!

To be accepted in the beloved, the beloved is our preference. If we have no beloved, then there are few expressions of love from us. We must love the humans we are now around. And to be accepted by them is our hope.

--21--

Torment. Shades of torment. Hues of torment. Metals of torment. And some humans thought it fun to talk of sadistic murder and sexual violence as sport. There are two real types of monsters: the archaic term that was once a term for a child with a birth defect; and a mentally insane violent adult.

The Nineteen-Sixties failed, leaving on a jet plane (as in black). Sweetness putrid now; serial murderers on the up and up. Only half way there, can we expect the gradual worsening, like the declines in virtue of the past? Think about it, just for a little while: exploitations, sadism, fascism, riches, luxury..." Down the toilet with the sixties; fifties; forties; thirties..."

Every man to his inheritance. Benefits listed added to grace. Punishments also according -- is what we do worth the inevitable effort to come? This is not karma, and this is not dogma; this is what we have felt, deep, in our heart we've felt.

The next fifty years may be a joke. The concentration of humanity at its all time peak, or like it was, "in the days of Noah." What a time to be born, when some think a nuclear explosion may be the only thing that is physically capable of dissolving their astral bodies. But the Numbers do not blur the Sympathies.

Some people have learned one lesson too many, or they have learned the Poison Lesson. This final lesson has left them inside the house -- permanently. It has caused them to fear new interactions with people. No type of real I-Thou relationships are ever established.

The postponement of the world of beauty is a very common painful event. You've got to understand, that when someone wants ethics and studies philosophy, with science and religion, and views it as a poet, or an artist of any type, many strange things will float into one's imagination. The amount of undocumented beauty becomes enormous.

It is so true that some of the insane are the ones who have seen strange, wondrous types of emotions, that burst the human mental frame, and that some of the geniuses are the ones who have seen these same strange strong types of emotions in doses that a human can handle.

Humans are of two types: the wheat and the chaff. The chaff crosses every boundary imaginable: color, class, education, religion, tastes in art, music and literature, knowledge of the physical sciences, political ideology. The chaff will make the future impossible. They are the goats who always rise to power and, in the guise of the wheat, kill the wheat.

The chaff are the ones who have denied us our toys, our family's securities. They are joyless robots or exploitive freaks. They are either poor, middle class, rich, or ultra-rich.

The wheat are the minority, although there are millions of them. They are scattered across the globe, as are the chaff. They might not know any other wheat nor even recognize themselves as wheat. The attempts of turning the chaff into wheat is perhaps some people's version of the Cause.

The trick in influencing human behavior for the better is to reinvent the same old moral lessons into a modern meaning.

The trick of creative production in this motivation is to ignore all the lies (everyone's) and to ignore all the conclusions (everyone's) -- to work out your twenty-eight volume encyclopedia, before it is too late. One day, it will be too late. Discipline is your lover.

Go back to your first impressions of such words as imagination, love, hate, and hope. Recapture the case history of your vocabulary's semantics.

Thinking in a mode of self-worth and greatness, when one goes to the library he looks with a healthy envy at the works of Newton, Kierkegaard, and Goethe. He understands that he is of their caliber. There is no stopping him, he must make a competent witness to the things that they made a witness to. He does it not out of "ego" or an ugly pride; he would rather live in another type of peaceful happiness. But something inside him is tearing him apart. He must be what this thing is telling him to be. All his life he felt that he would do something outstanding. He was taken out of the race of status with his peers. He was made to fall below so that he could ascend upwards instead of going horizontally. Some others, a hundred years from his death, would go horizontally on his plane. He had to look out for them; he had to protect their ground from others who would prepare a worse path.

All the thoughts of popular writers they'd never want you to know. Sitting back with a bottle they'd think, "Just doing this again and again like I have...I'll be one of greats one day!"

Who ever said this kind of thing? How much of world's thought came out of perfunctoraneousness, and not out of ethical and artistic necessity? How much of what we call our greatest thought was just the cyclical manifestation of reactionism?

Perhaps, the reason why there are so many mediocre poets, painters, singers, musicians, and the like, is that everyone is Trying To Do Everything Just Right -- everyone is trying to get the respect that their idols get from them. Well, they should try to get a few things wrong -- it will probably come naturally.

There are thousands of supreme poets that have died unheard. Their parents or spouses discarded their life's work like so much old newspaper.

I finally came to the point one day in my life when I knew no one could say to me:

"Young Man, as you leave the arts, literatures, and philosophies of the leisurely, go quietly. Take up with firm conviction and dedication the role of a bookkeeper, and, perhaps, one day you may be ready to do something such as a medical records specialist. Tell us nothing, please, just go quietly."

"No more ideas for operas, none have been made. No, you will not write the novel that has never been written, and which could never have existed without you. None of the things in the creative realm you will do

-- your fear of self-sacrifice has destroyed your opportunity."

"What is this world!" -- you scream after looking through the Help-Wanteds.

"I don't mind working. This is a dream, I can see what they mean now. What is the plan? I don't mind working."

How come some can see the end product of men's final product as a constant flux?

I am nothing; I am hidden. There is no statement that I must live up to. I have no audience; I have struck no pose. I am as I have always been; I have no intention for change. There are no mechanisms of compromise working on my craft. There is no competition, no, not in this day, not yet. Not until their full strength is encouraged by my work. I have incorporated my delusions of grandeur into reality.

I withhold so much, that is the key, for when minor flings occur, they have so much daring that they stand out.

"A faithful witness will not lie; but a false witness will! utter lies."

--22--

Meta-biology was not just a tangent to interest your fancy. There are seasons when I come back to this idea and examine all life anew in its scope. Just like many things that the immature see as dark or dangerous, and yet some see as fascinating, this is what meta-biology has become for me.

Cells are you and me; we are made up of them. Feel your cells: "Love to you, my brain cells. love to you, my bone cells. Love to you, my muscle cells. Love to you, my skin cells.

Intrinsic in this is a new way to feel, a shift, a progression in all future consciousness. You wouldn't smoke a cigarette or abuse your body in any other way because you would be belligerently hurting the Little Creatures that make up your body.

We all have our own little planet to play with, it is firmly lodged on the top of our necks. It is our head, or more accurately, I guess, it is our brain.

Various factions act out: "I want that slice of pizza in the refrigerator!"

"No, I don't need it. I've got to get to sleep."

I postulate a type of mechanical or chemical change: people start out as believers in God, this faith and trust in virtue causes them to not merely lead the animalistic lives they previously lived and this causes great intellectual development. Then, the people loosen their faith a little, and the way that this mechanism is fitted, very tightly, makes for much scientific gain to be made. The sieve is opened a little more, inventions are made more and more possible because people are motivated by the fact that they think they are getting away with something. This growth would not have been made without the beneficial and altruistic effects of the Christian faith.

The Neural Ganglion of the Earth was once concentrated on one continent, but as the mind of the Earth grew, as documented in the fact that Asians, the future American Indians, came across from Alaska into North America. Thoughts projected where the eyes and ears and other senses went, and where the brain was brought by the body. The Earth slumped in its orbit and marveled during those years. The thoughts of the Earth were surprising the Earth. The other planets that were alive and in an active stage of consciousness watched for the Earth's development.

The people played on the planet, games which only they could play. The people had no choice. The beacons for them in their cognition told them to never turn back. These beacons, microscopic as the antigens in our bodies, kept them on their programmed path.

The male and female of the humans were, out of all the cells of the Earth, the ones who were most capable of caring for each other. The biological impulses, which control the other animals so beautifully, are defeated by the humans in their complex pursuit of happiness.

Styles of architecture that repeat, such as the Greek or Roman styles, may be structures that are inevitable for man to create, i.e. structures that the planet needs, as our microbes create certain chemical compounds inside our body. The arrangement of our cities, canals, and farms may be precise to the genetic code of the planet.

Softened primates in a mall, down the arteries the cells travel. Smiling pretty cell-primates, human beings, Dick and Jane, consumers. As I look into the shopping mall, closely, I see that many are isolated, individuals, many others in groups of two. Each little shop is so vaginal; each shop with its goods and its salespersons. It is like a parasite/host situation, wherein the salespersons are trapped into this organization.

Styles of clothing, especially women's, tend to point toward the cellular regeneration of peripheral substances for planetary needs. Such similarities with any given century are apparent. Those who are more free can perhaps transcend styles, such as the way the street alcoholic does, or the way certain artists and writers transcend clothing styles. Older people retain certain semblances of their youthful clothing style. Exactly what function do various clothing styles play?

The restructuring of artificial limbs from wood to plastic and metal may show the fortification of the "microbial" levels, things may be getting stronger.

Is the interaction between bird life and human life vital in any way? Perhaps the fusing together of the small things, the "cells", is the only way that the small things can connect and become tissues.

Need it be said that I am just a cell and the art I seek to create is just a hormone for the health of the planet?

How is the genetic information stored in the creation and evolution of the new moon? How does the mother planet transfer its genes to the newborn planet? How are these genes arranged, since they must provide the information for humans, other mammals, fish, flower bearing plants, and others? How much does evolution play in the structure of the genetic material?

The planet perhaps can produce various types of moons, different species of moons may come out of the same mother planet, or that thing which is the stage between a planet and sun. Some moons may be dead. Will they ever live again? Some say celestial bodies reincarnate. What about human fears and hatreds, what purpose do they serve? What about the human domination of certain cells such as chicken, cows and pigs for food? How does this all come together?

The God of the Bible said the Earth was made for man, and that man was to rule over all the wild beasts. What exactly does this imply? Does this mean that man can murder them as he wishes, that he can consume as much animal flesh as desired?

What about our houses, our complete havens away from the wildlife of the elements? When we bulldoze the fields, are we constantly building platforms for the increase of our higher human ganglionic function, or are we only taking away from the holistic health of the planet?

And if the Earth can think for itself, how much is it to blame for the things that go wrong down here? Are the thoughts and decisions that the Earth has thought responsible for all the evil that goes on within its body? A parallel would be that of the man who makes decisions and actions that constantly make his cells, organs, systems work harder. Is this what the earth has been doing -- living a life of hedonism at our expense?

The people exercise to stay healthier -- do our body's cells exercise, so we will be healthier, or are we in control of that? We should have compassion on them, they try so hard!

Think of the scales tipping, feeling humor higher up, larger up; the size, a higher emotional as well as intellectual being. Its eyes shed a tear when you pray.

"Oh, cells of my body, virtue is love!" the dying last words of a man; a planet; a galaxy; a universe.

--23--

To write works of words that will rip into and awe the Hearts and Minds of Ladies and Gentlemen, without resorting to crude devices, but instead with purity and clarity, novelty and hope, mirth and cheer. To do the same with anything you care to create. Or take this as an analogy of life. It is an old idea; to change the world with art. Rectify and restore the ground lost by mistaken doctrines that have turned our youth into slaves of a prevalent cul-de-sac.

Please!

Have not too much respect for the culminative mind of mankind. Have only respect for what you can do with your own mind. Look not to books for the last word. Listen inside your past for what you've heard. Open all the doors when they do appear. Do not let faster thoughts come near.

Going to color pages quickly now with the fullness of sound I listen to on some of the music I own. I look at reality, at ultimate truth, as all days that have been actually sorted out for the benefit of all the Earth's children; economy of souls. The life of Earth is only: optimistic for all; pessimistic for some, optimistic for others; pessimistic for all. Choose one of these four.

The fields are more to the air than they are to me, because I can not contain them. The domesticated house cats see the cranium of the night sky with its stars more than I do, or have. The birds are getting a better supply of oxygen than me, because: I'm in a culture I didn't subscribe to; I'm on a diet of non-foods that my God did not want for me. Some revolt against a brick and mortar cage, but our revolt can also be against flesh and bone and skin. The cage is original sin; original skin.

Terrain poems, our reality present, compact with a view of Earth terrain. While we exist on land, we will be earthbound, but our needs need not bind us with tradition. If you cultivate the soil, it may be worth your while here -- success in your pursuit of happiness.

Smile of the terrain, of hill or field, mirror the various life forms -- transfer your consciousness. Examine thought with no language. Examine the stillness of the vegetation. Imagine your lifetime spent as moss on a tree trunk. Size is relative and is of no value where being is concerned.

Over treeless fields, I cuddle the terrain's nakedness: I am insane. Could we go far enough to say some ancient genetic trait is beaming through?

I see a bird type I've never ever seen before. It is tame on the thin tree branch ten feet in front of me. I stumble upon a box turtle and adopt it as a son for the day.

I cross over creeks on top of carcasses of trees. I squat near a small brook's light waterfall. I absorb the gentle cascade into my ears. Flowing into me, it stays where my head once was.

There are still many interesting things that can happen to us; things to look forward to. An optical oddity happened to me where all my sight turned purple; all objects lit by my vision had a purple tinge. You could look forward to this -- it just happened to me! And if it does happen to you, and you happen to be inside, quick! run outside! Look into the sky.

See the new clouds!

The Edict of your walk, blasted on trumpets in courtly Lindisfarne embroidery, the sunlight on leaves and the shadow of branches wetting the streets.

The Edict of pearl and gold -- it's mobile with you out of doors.

The Edict of staying outside, the Edict of sobriety -- the Edict of those who stay outside for long periods of time. We can unite with ancient ages, that the air and the sun are both then and now.

Our world would have been real beautiful, everyone an aristocrat at birth, and isn't that what everyone wants anyway? Everyone with a full education, a background in world travel, an appreciation of appreciation, the ability to appreciate -- others. We are all cared for, implicitly, we stay a while and rest, metaphorically drunk in the ages of our dreams. This is the soft reality that was purchased for us, just like a man purchases gifts when he courts his lady: the "bride and bridegroom" analogy in Christianity.

Inside my daily structure, I chose to begin to live inside of the structure. I chose to live beneath the structure's time mode, sequence; which is to say I will try to do whatever I please, while living a structured life.

New experience and a new hope, lots of books for reference.

Last month I got a fortune cookie that read: "Additional work will bring you new friends and more money." Yet, I can not afford to live anymore. I am the painter who must sell his brushes; the pianist who must sell his piano. All I can think is "Oh, well". All I can think is how I can enjoy myself. To visit the nice aquarium they built on the pier, or the zoo which fits in so nice with the suburbs.

It is always me that is to blame, for I have too few scars. Most of my brightest memories of daring and adventure took place in a four month period that is long gone.

I've got a lot of money coming to me eventually. This money is the events and the experiences or revelations of the day I die. When we die, we start out on a journey. All humans can be sure of this fact. What the journey is like, or where the destination is, I don't have many pretensions of knowing. We all have this lump sum coming to us. We will find out what is real, more than our endorphins can ever tell us. Of course we may get Alzheimer's disease, and have the cognition of a lump of jelly. If this happened then would we not be able to enjoy the scenery? Lord have mercy!

And one day you will die. This will be a very strange day. It most likely will have a morning and an afternoon when you will be awake. But will you understand, that this is the day you are to die? Will this day feel any different in any way, from any other day?

I want to sing about astronomy, but what is astronomy? It has been too long since anyone has asked that question. Ask the never known questions! I want to sing about astronomy (I should sing about geology). Astronomy is something else, something in addition to what we have done with the data. Astronomy is the corpsiest science that we have, yet it blossoms daily.

There is one thing that connects us/sustains us--hilarity. Something that is reckless.

I wish I could tell you of the future fun, to tell you of the new spring month, inventions of new surrealistic childhood, not dim at all in my feeling, but nonetheless a bit amorphous.

If the ninny-goats speak out their attack on hope, I must defend my hope, for hope is life. Hope is all we can use in our attack against useless logic. Logic is most deadly when it has no purpose, when it has no light to shine on something, yet it is still applied. Useless logic as such is only despairing. The anguish useless logic causes needs not to be our clothing, for we already have a set of clothes on. We looked at the useless logic trickle in, strain by strain, until all the "facts" were correctly calculated and we lost six-and-one-half ounces of liquid.

Hope is a varied beast; hope is the platypus. Hope is infinitely small at times, as in the presence of logic that is useless.

This is when we can utilize hope to combat useless logic. Digesting a minuscule bit of hope is all that we need to do to conquer despair.

Hope and faith are interwoven. Hope is the logic, the intellectual support for the faith. If you understand the science of hope then you will be ready to have faith in God. For the real artist or poet, hope is the first installment of life's awe; hope is the "A" volume of the intergalactic encyclopedia.

Although I've never had purple martins fight for me, the way of life is beyond elegy. At times it seems our realities equal an aviary. Who laid down the newspapers which we walk upon?

Are we eternal, or is my hope a lie? Is it a virtue? To sustain the time; only to keep us healthy for the health of the large organism we compose? Perhaps, perhaps, perhaps; vanity of vanities. Are we at the end? Is this the most damnable of heresies? I don't need the fame for it, I don't need the sin for it, and I only need to be close to salvation.

Visionaries' land of adolescent masterpieces of original lives, together in a building forever they can stop time. People who don't get embarrassed. People who were meant to live in isolations (of a sort) for a better distribution of their frequency. See how they have love in their habit. These are the beautiful people that you will run into perhaps twenty in your lifetime. On the street; in the shopping malls. Passive parts of common parts that are evil when active, as with some of the rich who are collectively to blame for the world's condition, due to the fact that they are the ones who have made all the decisions throughout time (but we don't wrestle with flesh and blood, but with powers and so forth).

It has been too long since I've had that beautiful face on, since I've looked out from a beautiful face, a majestic look, yes, majestic. It is a childhood and adolescent look few can carry it over into adulthood for fear of being called conceited, idiotic, effeminate -- if you're a guy, or perhaps even insane. The smell of flowers in the air. There is no other like the days in May, and its hours around six thirty PM. This is when the evaporated chemicals float in the air that is ever new in its lighting.

--24--

The Grocery Store of vacationing years spent, kinetic gifts of time as a substance, purchases of things that exist in this full-blown manifestation of the virtuous universe. We exist in low stages, in a crude mixture of the Virtuous Universe, giving of our bad vibes which jumble their own signals and beach on the Scurry Islands.

We have been given tickets, formed by a conscious desire, created by love. I don't argue facts.

One day in the past we had breathed in love. Verily, one day that was our average. Today and days since then we believe that Jumble Fair is good indeed, and we sunbathe in the burnlight on the beach.

The packages from the shopping malls in the clearer image of our virtuous universe maternally beckon to us, to tell us that the universe is virtuous, to us, as we are virtuous to all of it.

A grown up now, I did make that transition, people can accomplish their own desire, regardless of complications. An orthodox middle-of-the-road discipline is what it took to turn the trick. It didn't have to take increased malice. Some things manifest themselves so much stronger to me, some early Nineteen-Seventies pop songs, some foods, some weather conditions. I have preferences -- this is for sure. The point is not that I think I should avoid my preferences, it's that I wonder if I'll ever get my fill of them.

I've still misused my time, since Earth Terror shook me at fifteen. I should have obeyed the harsh sayings of Christ. Yes, boys and girls, be faithful to the lifesaver. Don't jump off high bridges. Put trust in being alone again. Be faithful to the lifesaver.

There never... will there ever be the days when we have skies shining upon the future? We all around, never a Them. Perhaps after four-hundred years of individuals changing. Will They someday act towards the way which each present dreamer sees perfection? Will it ever be connected consciousness? No one likes their loneliness. I see a networking that will obliterate the impression of "overpopulation" being harmful. Have all of us been on a progress to a nearer perfection? Do we just waste away and dream towards the stupid goal of a moneyless horizon?

Is the love of perfection the root of all evils? Is the love of the common evil of humanity the only way to find the good in life? They never know the truth-less isolation, the girl-less me, the money-less child. I never really needed God to hold my hand when I had my aims and God became one. There never is a mostly content seeker after perfection. Why can't I dissolve and ubiquitate? I've been on the path of the Yogi, the Christian, the Theosophist, and still others, and I have gathered one thing: if there is no one coming from above down to me, or to all men in all time, and if there is no one or nothing besides ourselves who hears the thoughts we think, or prayers we pray, then we are truly alone, with a maze of demons, angels, saints, criminals, and children. We are floating in an anarchistic sports arena. And then is extreme caution more important than trust?

There are ways to break through the repetitive days because there must be. Examples of this are such things as serious meditations, prayer, out of body experiences, and angelic visitations. With the exclusion of prayer, these things can be the most dangerous non-fatal activities on earth.

We must break through to the noumenal. All factual things on earth seem to concern things of no eternal importance. All things of eternal importance to our lives seem at first to be taken by faith. But these faithful images illuminate all aspects of our life. The range of being on earth is so vast: from the child molester to the saint. Is heaven and hell the outcome of this?

If we start from Point A, that is, if our birth is our first appearance anywhere then all is excusable -- the Earth is both the breeding ground and the test department. But, if you believe in reincarnation, and you look at the wide range of human souls, then you have to realize that this is only one sphere of existence. There are worlds both lower than our low, and worlds higher than our high.

You may say that there are only higher worlds than ours. I don't believe any sane individual would say that there are only lower. Perhaps our world is like all other worlds. It says in the Bible: "For God so loved the world" -- notice that the word "world" is singular. Jesus said he had other flocks of sheep. The usage of "world" should be read as "this world" to our astronomically opened eyes.

To believe that our world of life/death is the only world of life in the universe is not as preposterous as it seems. I am against the idea that it is the only one, although I can not say that I believe in more worlds of life as I can say I believe in God. Belief in God and belief in extra-terrestrial life are two separate species of faith.

The reasons why life may only exist on Earth are:

A) That may be all the Creator desired

B) He may have set up the billions of galaxies for an unknown needed physical, astronomical or even astrological relationship related to the myriad of souls on earth.

C) It may have been just as easy and yet prettier to create millions of galaxies.

D) To create only one solar system may have looked absurd.

In those billion trillion stars we see, shall we hope to be special, like a child's love for the Easter Bunny or Santa Claus -- a constant dependence? Some things are much larger and have more brain cells; it's possible everything is special.

Yes, I can believe, because I leave the answers bright to the dark questions; I do not scurry to answer the questions myself. I am still a sinner, and, furthermore, existentially, this is all fiction my friend. Of the matter concerning God, it seems He is both a higher emotional and intellectual being than myself. He could easily care for a trillion planets with a billion souls piece. I do not limit all of existence; all of that which will ever be.

Although, here is an attempt:

All there is in the whole of being existence is a billion, 142 mile long series of consciousness inversions, mathematical expressions with senses replacing the variables.

All there is to all there ever is are virtues piling up on one another, multiplying themselves by themselves until the fission occurs and the brightness travels farther and farther outward and outward into a big chamber of Inside-It.

All there ever is to the universe of creation is all things that we have seen awake and asleep. Inside the objects themselves, we must dissect all representation and lightning fast processes.

Yes, dissect and sit back and watch the perceptions bloom.

All there ever is to God Himself is all there ever will be to us, and this is biblical.

I will always be crawling after that peace of mind childhood contentment, which breeds the bliss of a hundred emotions after creation of ascetic splendors. I will always run away from stress pain... pain gotten from being long gone from being content from sitting on a public lawn, like we achieved so easily as a child. Without courage, verily, all is lost.

I dreamed the misfortune to be born an energy cell, a simple mortal human, a device in a clockwork that needs my nervous energy and fear towards death, for the heat and combustion of the machine. That is, like you, sometimes I feel that I was born to die. And I see that what is required for me to do is not my heart's craft. For we are not in the age of patrons nor appreciation. I smile at the artless persons, the business arts persons, the artness persons who navigate trend and air traffic control style. I see art works from the past, forgotten to the avenues of exposure, and I realize that no matter how "good" I am, I do not wish to be so rude to eclipse other isolated souls who are my siblings.

Popular impeccable packaging, which cost thousands to get right, spent in so many directions, all pointing away from essence. The only thing left to do for those who feel like this is . . . is to write your eight-hundred page autobiography. It would be a joy that you are well worth, my siblings.

For centuries, artists have been contributing to the joy of the human world. The simple fact is that the human world has not often contributed to the joy of the artist. Most artists that have furthered art have been ridiculed. The revenge that God gives the artist is that the artist makes changes in the direction of humanity. The time when the world should be kind to the artists, poets, and other creative types is the time when severe problems are arising. By handing these problems over to impartial extremely creative types, who would respect nationalisms, and consider their recommendations, the Earth may transcend the stage it is in. (And perhaps by setting up an international demagogue confinement squad, further safeguards will be established).

Should I be the one to cry? Mankind has always been led down into dungeons, (or is it led done into dungeons?) I am certain that God also made pestilence so that man would not get too egotistical. Hope is unavoidable, or is that inevitable?

When all this crap is lost and I return to my love, return to all just jello and blue, to all just my genes, of a tribal sub-consciousness... is that what we need to do? But do you see what I am leading up to? Personified idealisms, a population of them. "Life" -- do you need it? Does it need you? Were the Buddhists somehow right? Should we evaporate our will's driving power; should we just be a good householder, and float around and let death shoot a hole in the boat's bottom?

Alternate landscapes beckon my preference. I deplore my current climate and topography. I dream of Arizona, of the hot, with dry winds – a strange dream about cacti.

While we are here awake, as functioning machines made out of protoplasm and cell walls, we play the role we are required (by ourselves or the unknown) to play. We are our own Eros, we broadcast; some things interfere on our own will, but we do not interfere on anything's will higher than ours.

What is compassion for if we only compare it to dust? The fuel of the will is suffering into gain. When you're halfway in the middle the two never look the same.

I just heard a little boy say "Oh volleyball, that's fun!" He said it like it was sacred, like it was something the big people do. How sad. But what else is there to do but be eternal and play volleyball? Volleyball thus becomes as important as anything else if we are eternal.

--25--

Sometimes your bubble gum mind wears thin. You are thinking that it is O.K. to stay inside today, because no one will have fun today -- it's raining. Do you recall watching polarities at a young age? You did, you know. Your brain was just as active and you looked out then as you observe this Today. You were smoother and you didn't notice the trespassing of the very laws you yourself set up. And I believe in this case stereotypes are appropriate to the general scene.

Feelings are big thoughts and philosophies are small thoughts. I feel that which I thought closer to the childhood age stronger than what I think about now. "She's just a girl." equals "us boys", when it actually meant something. Like getting numbed to statements such as "He got eaten by an alligator," when said on a television comedy show, and when it could really mean something to you. I do see good things in old thoughts; thoughts that are so old they take ten to twenty minutes to remember.

Of God, of virtue, of sunshine, of prolonged human relationships, of altruistic grocery shopping, of inexpensive benevolent tourist traps.

Of God, of Eternity, of experimentation. Of those on Earth who have broken down and broken free, not just broken down and then broken up.

Of the laboratory of the child mind's memory in your head. Of the decision, even if we are just fragile cells, to be all that there is to virtue, to be all that there is to enjoyment, by ourselves, with others.

To isolate ourselves in blissful durations of the write, strenuous sobriety of monastic spring days, laying on a blanket on the grass, or if possible, on the beach, with a million other forms of worlds available, like in the outside world, where the floor has depth and we can think: thirty miles down and it will still be there.

Earth life can be a joy at times. Part of the difference toward the preferable world is the stifling of eighty-five percent of the thoughts which spring up in one's mind, so one may be able to be still, and hear the words of the abstract, the common Lord of mankind, the friend of our childhood.

Wild in blue splashes sparkles the eventide near horizons which are multi-layered. Candle-like objects burn. We huddle. Other journey's crisp threads in strong memory possibilities. Possibilities must be in your habit. They evaporate further in -- into the treey woods and fauna, vegetation covered by sky.

A thousand birds will cross my trail; some species come only once in a lifetime. The lovers' trails echo around, sometimes in the alternative of all that haste and waste. Keep on echoing, dear trails. We may wander in when you are more genuine than the hats which have been so neatly taken down and set in place for us.

I could see the overflow of my questions to be unwise, produced by perhaps biology? Ego-scores? The moon? I gave Christ garbage, now I must promise to give Him asceticism to help clear the ganglionic trails which sin has etched.

We don't need drugs to tell us about the purple haze. An appropriate science spirit occurred as the disciplined version of the energy of the thirty years from 1845 to 1875, something that may have caused Rimbaud's doctrine of the disillusionment of the senses. This was the dawn of the first Surrealism in France, those that sought to fuse the unconscious with the conscious. In what way is the derangement of the senses related to science? Is it the opposites that we should seek? As art becomes formless, do the arts of science pick up its form? Or was it in the haziness of our seeing the real world of the senses that we then could imagine the greatness that could be of science, and in naming it, we began to create it?

We need not drugs to see the new science, the science that's cheap, that's purple, that, to some, is like the euphoria they so desperately can't find sober so they attribute it to drugs. The science that is not a fool's religion. We need not drugs to make us feel alive; an examination of "insanity" could be much more potent. What we really need is certain types of asceticism and prayer, which give us the philosophical finality, and take us away from the frequent harsh changes, and move us toward the God which we hope is there.

Who is the keeper of the righteous indignation? Why is it left here to warp our minds? Why do we have to go from indignation to asceticism? What part does humor have to play in indignation? Is indignation only valid when it concerns unjust treatment of others, or can we be indignant about the way we are treated?

Watering your world like a circling sprinkler, dropping gobs of purity. Tonight you'll sleep on leafy green, made by the genetic vegetation artist. I'm sorry the future is burning brighter; I am sorry to know what progress is. The rhythm track of the sprinkler, must keep me out of resting in any sense of pain; making stumbling efforts not to rest in pain. Some need something like an indoor swimming pool to disengage their whatevers, until they're ready for ascetics to pull them out of someone else's sanity.

There are other rhythms which I've dreamed of -- clicking blue glass with ocean roar -- which seem like they would recharge us, so that we could drop gobs of purity on each other and the question factory would not have enough momentum to send the questions rising to the surface.

-26-

Wondrous Huge Creature, digesting its coarse body into lighter by the life of its creatures within. Spectacular picture of highest organism becoming itself by self-contained evolution, plus energy from the sun. The generations of millions of species of animal-cells and millions of species of plant-cells, appearing and disappearing over a hundred billion years. (Who do you think you are?).

I give to You, Lord, my mind, a piece of my life (of my whole life in faith and sacrifices -- small, yet, I've changed my world for You). I give You thus my thought. Speak to me in Your own tongue. True, my dedication is not as strong as that of others, but You have seen it when it was. Be kind to me without my effort, so I may repay Your glory, and want to serve You. The stretches are not ever fatal.

Corrupting my mind with the entertainment of the status-quo -- their information is dangerous; their information is wrong. Darkening my dream with the ways of Man. Just a creature and a creator; there are no men here, nor man's history. I am no one besides me. I drain off more information every day. In my box of personalities, in an existential way, I am only one part of me. God the creator is there with me. His presence redefines the word "security." And His essence is not artificial at all.

When we have described inscapes and out, and seemingly exhaust all interest in the peripheral, in the peripheral which had originally destroyed interest in the virtuous, perhaps then a new poetry can begin, which would be beyond all our present feelings and ideas. The way we would do this is to realize a singular reason for us does exist, and for any question, there will always be an answer to our prayers and questions.

This is given if we want to get out of the stupor. This is the problem the peripheral has created: the denial of a problem. And what is this problem, this stupor, in even more detail? It is this: if we took ten questions that mankind could never be certain about the infallibility of the answers, the problem would deny the hope that we would ever know the answers or even that the answers don't exist, so that the questions would not be given any attention.

Will we never be certain about absolute answers, only absolute questions?

Open up the glorious good in your days. It is not artificial at all. The good inside you is always there. Never think it has to be fabricated.

Open right up the glorious good in your days; it's not artificial at all! God is the Wisdom House. He knows all things, such as why life is goodness (the ultimate in enigmas?). The stars fill empty space! He knows! Put them there for a reason.

God -- the Wisdom House. Happy hymns create more holidays. Wedding bells commence the feast. Bride and groom dissolve need for priest.

God is the Wisdom House -- every effect, He knows the cause. When in doubt, you've made the delay; the delay from the quickness of the Spirit.

Hope, sky, and the surf drifts by. Cleave to a warm day's try. Speak now watch night falling. Open up relations calling. Spoken gift seeks myth ago. Christ's love separates regrets. Rich, poor, pretty, ugly; a day's work gives you your reality. And the paycheck is your Paris.

After thinking about such things, it seems a true renaissance person would be adept at sex, too. Frequent spins of outside fair grounds. Romance, a major motivation, or a major cause? We are apart always more than we are together. The current problems of male/female relationships are a great example of dark humor gone deadpan. Why doesn't God connect all the male with female? Who really knows the ins and outs of gender sins?

The street riots in the street. The street riots in the shopping malls. The street riots on the beaches. The street riots in the school halls. The street riots in the temples. There is no literature that will end the street riots of hate and street riots of power envy. Do I have to tell you, now that the literary device has become apparent, that the term "street riots" is only metaphorical? An early disclosure might have taken something away from a climatic revelation at the end of the book, that may have driven the idea home in a more powerful way, but I'd risk making the rest of the book obscured and subordinate, which is not my intention.

One day, when I was watching you riot on the street, a strange street person came up to me and said, "I saw a society where it grows upon people to have the child become father to the man. There were many things in this society that were weird, like this was actually like a utopia. Somehow, without spoiling the kids, they let them grow up and find what they would enjoy the most, and they have been doing it like this for thousands of years. Everyone had total freedom, but they seemed to help everyone else out. But the funny thing was that no one really needed help too bad, since they were born into this society where more or less they were helping each other out for thousands of years.

"Anyway, they talked about this thing which was a substance that a child is born with that he can gradually lose by it being smashed down by his culture. It was sort of something like what we call curiosity, from what I gather. So the way they were, the kids did not have to be forced to learn, they were just doing what they wanted to do..."

When minds are fresh, they can always absorb fresh air. When minds are fresh, free from drugs and despair, or an ego-score -- then they can absorb fresh air.

Did you ever get the feeling that what you were doing was just too important, that the words that you had to speak or write, the philosophy that you had to disclose, came from a higher source, and somehow you could barely trust yourself to get it done, hardly trust your mortal self with the utterances safety?

Are we all here for the culmination of the Earth, here to make art for this final period of our metabiological function in the Earth's life? Frightening information is presented to humanity. We enhance this final period to a naked index of truth. Like a soft-core novel, with a terrifying last three pages, the earth ends its gastrula stage and is bursting open.

I see my ultimate revenge, if the need be, on the concept of the exploitative universe as two-fold: philosophy and virtue. Many people have the feelings that life may end with this life, everything thus seeming so unfair, and they take out their anger in imaginations of violence or actual violence and debauchery. For me, philosophy and virtue works better. Meta-biology is such a hardcore philosophy contrived by man that it gives me a certain feeling above mundanity. Virtue is the harshest protest against the conclusions of the biological-sociological Pseudo-Darwinian atheistic worldview. Violence and debauchery will only take you so far and then put you in the opposite direction, but virtue takes you to a farther extreme.

"Wasting time when one could be writing books about how one feels, I see my ego as being the part of me that wants to be in the Encyclopedia Britannica. I've always wanted to be in there. Is that skill or ego?"

Art thoughts are big thoughts. Art thoughts are how to see beauty, big thoughts about big beauties, symbiotically produced. Love's thought color pages now, too. Love is a feeling art form, that is to say, that the feeling of love is an aesthetic feeling. We hope to get more of these right. They are the best thoughts to remember.

We've got to decide to combine or extract. Whichever one will provide more information, or do we try to fit in with the style? Some things are impossible. Our intellects are different from those of only fifty years ago — we are wise asses, but what of those fifty-years from now? The next stage that we have prepared the groundwork for is living in the world apart from the pages of malicious self-serving classification.

All aspiration toward creativity in the arts is channeled towards creativity in the virtues. I am presented with only one ounce of the thousands and thousands of tons of human misery that goes on behind closed, closed doors, far, far away from any television camera. I want to take that ounce and reroute it back into the soul from which it came and try hard to help it look out into the world with its own intrinsic dignity. It not artificial at all!

To be creatively virtuous, the oldest good idea there was among the strangers whom your life depended on. To be creatively virtuous, something stronger than idea, but weaker than reality. I gladly abandon all the small trappings of the radical -- only in potential towards insult or violence -- subculture of my existence's year span. I dive into the waves of the will of God, and body surf in the times of divine organization.

I have never had any problem separating church and state, I'll just have to work on separating church and virtue. But for the truth, which prepackaged cipher-script do I choose? I must choose the one that has been somatically encoded. I will use this faith until the glass that I see darkly through is shattered into forgotten yet dangerous shards.

-27-

Have you discerned the Cause that rings throughout this book? Literally, a thousand jeweled pages encased in a sculptured binding of nonexistent metals. These sentences contain juices of a planet's fruits grown from salvation's ground. Once there was in everyone's mind a religion without any problems. Parts of it were eaten by hosts who had their way of life at stake. It is still there to be found, but the excavation of the first sedimentary layers for some is difficult.

The end of my days will present the single inevitability, existing externally, which will devour me for better or worse. The end of all our days will provide one as such. The jewelry of my highest thought was produced out of the highest, direst needs: observing holy religion and righteous logic.

Preserving to the utmost the pursuit of saintly hedonism, enjoyment is when our keys start the engine. I sustain the vision and observe it.

Can you see still, He is pulling you out of it. There is nothing for granted, this is all we're doing now. By your faith you can show Him you are prepared to take a chance. If you make too small of an effort, it's not going to work right. The word gospel means "good news," meaning something that can keep one in happiness. So the key to the song is the key of our hearts; it is about one thing that has been with us from the start.

What do you think of God? What does anyone know of God? Just a simple offering of help, and a warning that some kind of damnation will follow a life too far out of line with magnificence. Can you see the common sense behind that? It is a good thing that the unsaved (define the term for yourself!) deserve to go to somewhere else when they die. The "unsaved" are obviously the ones who have screwed up Earth for this long. This must mean that Heaven is a very exceptional place! Hell fire may only be the current hell fire in an unethical Earth life carried out to its logical conclusions in eternity. Except that the good people would not be there to help them out like they have been on earth. Obliteration would be better.

Subtract from this what you will; would you like a Joker King God, a God who is only in it for our fun? That could be the icon in times of trouble. Subtract from it what you will.

The music goes on for a long time. Icicles of ornamental white dancing percussive notes. The lyricism is hard to catch on to. It sings of summer and lawns and sprinklers. In my beginning, I was unleashed in the presence of those with love. In their creative eyes, I've chosen to let it begin again. Last week this happened.

All these years, Lord, you know it has been real. All the hurt, the hope, the insanity, leads me to You. The aesthetic religion of Christianity is all my love can hold on to. Let the pessimists be forgotten! Soldiers of doubt, drawing the bow of ideas born of vain words and flinging arrows of decrepit worthlessness.

I can't see Jesus' salvation in the eyes of every man's acceptance. I can only see the love I have been shown, and I can't refuse such salvation. What else could there be other than love? There are only otherwise polemics against spirituality and a solution for it, and both by children of misguided disobedience. What else is there but God and man, or neither, but something much more complicated?

Nothing needs to be done in areas that I see lacking. What I could provide would be great, but that which is salvation for me, is not what I could provide for you. (Hand in hand, is what some say -- too much for me, something to someday be?). Don't need to go down for the books that cry out to be written. There is dreaming and deceit. Self-indulgence, slothfulness, and more dreaming and deceit. Are we going to die in our original enthusiasm, or are we like the types who are like the flowers, and fade?

Finality in one's own life. The theme of all good work; the Cause for which I am motivated. The philosophic finality of truth unobjectionable. The meaning of our being here, the discernment or revelation of the true God. With these things we will have achieved finality, and found truth (food) of a lasting and higher nature. Completion of seeking and crystallization of individuality. Once and for all: objective understanding.

There is a kid, a fourteen year old, in Tennessee, who is going to find out the meaning of life. He is an example. There is a little girl in Spain, who wants to find out the meaning of existence. She, too, is an example -- of the reason we are here.

I've heard from one who denies the value of any type of motivation for the cause. This person said at one time he was motivated, but he now no longer cares; he no longer sees any value in being "idealistic," (as he calls it!). Obviously, he can not detect, nor has he stayed with his "idealism" long enough to detect its pragmatism. It is only available for those who earn it; for the free.

So my advice is to the reader who is affected is that there is always correction, that is, that when you stop praising the universe, then you've died, and don't tell the ear of the universe, God, anything different.

Truth is life, being in virtue is truth. To act on truth without understanding it is better than merely understanding it and not acting. Were our brains not made to understand the full truth? Is it impossible for us to explain truth by that which is seen around us daily? Better, if the Above gradually explained it to us.

Pretending the yesterdays are on show in a jar, out on a table where professors bring their young wives. Opening the pages of a far away star, leave those pages empty dear and you lose where you are.

In successive durations of now exists our life, the constant on and off of what we really want. We are living. I am glad you are here. Isn't it amazing the living that God is giving? Isn't it love?

I hope to be able to love you; the infinite you that I meet everyday while we riot on the streets. True love is my object for all the prayers. Stay next to me. Never leave for too long. You are great! I will always need to be with you.

Have you discerned the Cause that rings throughout this book? The desire for the convulsive, for objective insight, for the past? Have you discerned the facts of the battle? Have you declared a truce?

Other Books Written by R.S. Pearson

Virtuism: Philosophy and the Aesthetics of Virtue
The Experience of Hallucinations in Religious Practice
Hyperreligiosity: Identifying and Overcoming Patterns of Religious Dysfunction
Exhausting the Interaction of Words: Computer-automated Brainstorming with the ParaMind Program ($19.95)
Grandiosity and the Empowerment of the Spiritual and Artistic (to be published in late 2007)

Each book is $14.95 except where noted. Please include $4 postage for each book in the U.S., and $11 for international shipping per book. You can also visit us on the web at www.telicalbooks.com

Make checks out to Telical Books and mail to:

Telical Books
P.O. Box 27401
Seattle, WA 98165-2401
U.S.A.

- -

Order Form

Name____
Address______________________________________
____
City____
State___________ Postal Code____________________
Country______________________________________